THE CREATIVE
BOOK OF
KITES

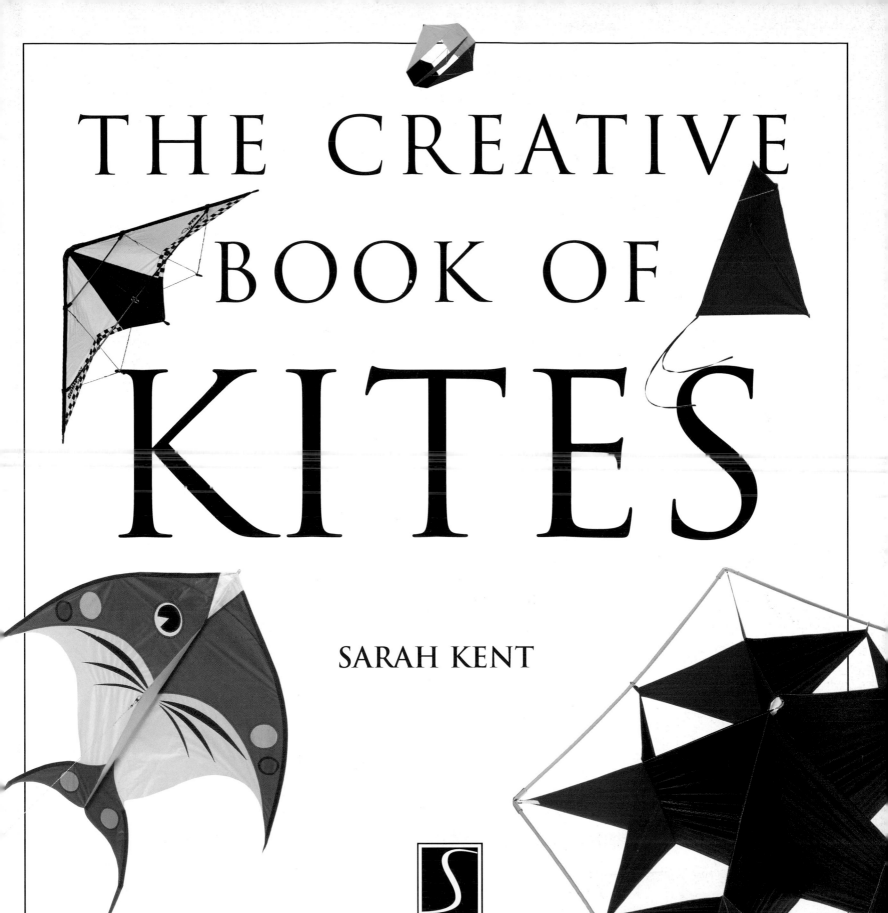

THE CREATIVE
BOOK OF
KITES

SARAH KENT

SMITHMARK

Commissioning Editor: Will Steeds
Produced for CLB International by The Design Revolution,
Brighton, England
Project Editor: Margot Richardson
Design: Lindsey Johns
Illustration: Ian Loats, Vanessa Good
Photography: APM Studios, Brighton
Production: Neil Randles, Ruth Arthur, Karen Staff
Color reproduction: HBM Print Pte., Ltd., Singapore

CLB 4887
© 1997 CLB International

This edition published in 1997 by Smithmark Publishers,
a division of U.S. Media Holdings, Inc.,
16 East 32nd Street, New York, NY 10016.

SMITHMARK books are available for bulk purchase
for sales promotion and premium use. For details
write or call the manager of special sales,
SMITHMARK Publishers,
a division of U.S. Media Holdings, Inc.,
16 East 32nd Street, New York,
NY 10016; (212) 532-6600

Produced by CLB International
Godalming Business Centre
Woolsack Way, Godalming, Surrey, UK

ISBN 0-7651-9493-7

Printed in Italy

10 9 8 7 6 5 4 3 2 1

Acknowledgments

The author would like to thank the following for
their much-valued help with the preparation of this book:
Mark Cottrell, The Kite Store Ltd., Paul Thody and Estelle Barton,
Air Born Kites, Carl Robertshaw, Airkraft, Jeremy Boyce,
Airkraft/High As A Kite, Felix Mottram, The Decorators, Tony
Ferraro, In-4-Mation, Top Of The Line, Sport Kites, Revolution
Enterprises Inc., and all those listed below who kindly
contributed illustrations and photographs.

Bibliography

If you wish to learn more about kites and kite-flying,
the following books are recommended:
Pelham, D. 1976. *The Penguin Book of Kites.*
London, Penguin Books.
Yolen, W. 1976. *The Complete Book of Kites and Kite Flying.*
London, Simon & Schuster.

Contents

Right: *1985 World sport-kite team champions "Airkraft." Left to right: Jeremy Boyce, Nik Boothby, James Robertshaw, and Carl Robertshaw flying Top-Of-The-Line North Shore Radical kites in formation.*

Introduction

For more than two millennia, the kite has been an international symbol of childhood joy, for many of us, fulfilling the dream of flight by proxy.

Throughout their colorful history, kites have appeared all around the globe, adopting guises as diverse as the indigenous cultures found within each continent. Since the first simple bird-like aerodynes were constructed in China, humankind has manipulated the kite form to produce a plethora of weird and wonderful flying objects.

Twentieth-century technology has accelerated this development, and consequently we now have kites with dimensions that extend to hundreds of yards or meters, as well as steerable aerofoil kites capable of traveling through the air at speeds exceeding 100 miles (160km) an hour! Using new materials such as ripstop nylon and carbon fiber, the artists and craftsmen of the kite world continue to create their flights of fantasy: some to decorate the skies at a growing number of international kite festivals; others to complement the skills of a new generation of sport-kite fliers.

The **Creative Book of Kites** takes a detailed look at an area in which art, myth, and symbolism meet aeronautical science and technology. This exploration of tethered wings introduces us to some of the crafters, hobbyists, and sportsmen and women who dedicate themselves to the pursuit of the perfect flight and demonstrates an easy way for the reader to get involved.

A brief history

◆

Kites have evolved in a
huge variety of forms over an
estimated 2,500 years.
Through the centuries they have
proliferated worldwide as a result
of exploration and trading to
become familiar features of many
diverse cultures. This brief history
relates their passage through
time to the present day.

A brief history

Since the beginning of time, man has dreamed of bird-like flight; a dream that is manifest in texts and illustrations dating right back to 500 B.C. It is not known precisely where and when the first kite was flown, but it is popularly held that the Chinese led the way with early aerodynes copying the form of birds. It is certain, however, that more than two millennia before Isaac Newton discovered the force of gravity, the invention of kites was already fueling mankind's desire to defy it.

Although the earliest accounts of kite flying seem to center around the Far East and Egypt, kites embarked on a worldwide odyssey following ancient trade routes. In this way they were adopted on virtually every continent, acquiring new forms and mythologies as they entered different cultures.

KITE MYTHS AND LEGENDS

One popular Chinese legend tells of a farmer whose hat was blown off by a gust of wind as he toiled in a paddy field. Intrigued by the ability of his headgear to fly, he retrieved it and attached it to a length of twine, thus creating the first kite. Another early account describes a wooden framed, bird-shaped kite built and flown in China around 500 B.C.

Kite flying became a hugely popular pastime in China, inspired by the festival of Ascending on High, an event that has taken place each year for hundreds of years. It is celebrated on the ninth day of the ninth month, as this was the day on which an entire family had been saved from peril by their love of kites. On the eve of this fateful day, a father dreamed that catastrophe would befall his family. Not knowing quite what action to take to avert the premonished doom, this wise and placid man took his wife and children to a quiet spot in the countryside where they spent what might have been their final hours happily indulging in kite-flying, their favorite pastime. On returning home that evening, they found that sure enough, their house had collapsed, destroying all they had possessed. The simple act of flying a kite had spared them from being buried amid the rubble, and thereafter was celebrated by thousands as an exceedingly fortuitous way to spend the same date.

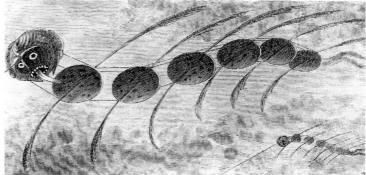

Above: *An early Chinese centipede kite. Some kites of this type include hundreds of disks in their construction.*

Left: *Elaborately decorated bird kites flock on high in this oriental flying scene.*

Always vehicles for the imagination, kites themselves have inspired many diverse feats. It is said that in 169 B.C. a Chinese general, Han Hsin, flew a kite over the walls of a palace, using the length of its string to gauge the distance that his troops would have to tunnel in order to enter this enemy territory surreptitiously.

LIFTING MEN

In A.D. 1282, the explorer Marco Polo gave his own account of enormous kites being used by Chinese sailors to lift terrified men from the decks of ships. The success or failure of this operation was taken as an augury for the planned voyage.

Early Japanese prints bear testament to similar feats of man-carrying. One depicts the son of Minamoto-no-Tametomo, an ingenious Samurai warrior, being flown from his island of exile lashed to the sail of a huge rectangular Edo kite. These acts of man-lifting foretold a much later time when nineteenth-century aeronautic pioneers, such as Samuel Franklin Cody, would use kites as a basis for experiments in early forms of aviation.

KITES IN JAPAN

It is believed that the first kites to arrive in Japan were brought there by Buddhist missionaries in around A.D. 700, during the T'ang Dynasty. These kites probably held profound religious significance, as many types of kite throughout the world do still. After all, there is no simpler expression of transcendence so appropriate to a multitude of philosophies.

On May 5 each year, every Japanese household to which a son has been born flies a windsock in the form of a carp. The celebration, known as Boys' Festival, is also an occasion to fly magnificently hand-painted kites. This echoes the Korean practice of inscribing kites with the name and date of birth of each male child. These are flown to the furthest extent of the string, then released to drift far and free on the wind, bearing away any evil spirits that might otherwise hinder the child in his future years.

Japanese ingenuity soon gave rise to more practical reasons for flying kites. They even became tools of the high-rise building trade as hoists for carrying materials aloft to craftsmen engaged in the construction of towers. Certainly,

Japan has a rich and diverse kite culture. Almost every region has its own unique design, one of the best known being the Nagasaki Hata. Minute by comparison with the giant Edos, this kite measuring about 1ft (30cm) square was adapted from Indian fighter kites introduced to Japan in the early 1540s by Western European traders.

Left: *Some of the thousands of carp windsocks flown from flagpoles in celebration of Boys' Day in Japan.*

FIGHTING IN THE SKY

By way of contrast to more ethereal flying urges, kite fighting is dynamic, exhilarating, and requires vigorous cunning. The object of a kite fight is to cut your opponent's string. Achieving such a victory requires a combination of sheer skill and copious amounts of ground glass or porcelain stuck to the kite string using a paste made from rice or egg white. One form of Japanese fighting kite is the six-sided Rokkaku. This type can still be found doing battle in the skies over many international kite festivals at the hands of teams of three or more pilots clad in distinguishing garb.

Kite fighting also became a popular alternative sport in Malaysia, Korea, and Polynesia, where it flourished alongside religious flying ceremonies.

TRENDS IN THE PACIFIC

Polynesian folklore tells of such a contest between the two wind gods, Rongo and Tane. These sparring brothers flew in airborne combat, soaring and diving, until suddenly the tail of Tane's kite became ensnared in the branches of a tree. This, in kiting terms, was the end of the road for Tane, and Rongo, the elder, was proclaimed winner. The battle for supremacy in the skies has long been reenacted by the people of Polynesia, where the highest kite is said to be endowed with the victorious spirit of Rongo.

In Malaysia, before recorded history, kites were flown to appease the gods who preside over the monsoon. In secret ceremonies, hundreds of small palm-leaf kites were offered up on coastal breezes to quell the powerful and often destructive seasonal typhoons.

Beyond their spiritual or combative role in the southern Pacific region, kites have long been a part of the essential human tool kit for survival. For centuries, fishing has been the main industry of the Malay and Polynesian archipelagos, and kites have played a vital role in bringing home the catch. These fishing kites are simple constructions of leaf sails supported by bamboo frames. Their purpose is to carry a fishing line out beyond shallow coastal waters, without casting ominous shadows or disturbing the water's surface. The same artful method is sometimes used by anglers in other parts of the world.

THE GREEKS

Although it is widely believed that kites originated in the Far East, there is evidence to suggest that the ancient Greeks explored tethered flight independently. As far back as 400 B.C., records describe a flying object which became known as the Dove of Tarentum. This was the invention of a scientist named Archytas and was, as its name implies, derived from the study of birds in flight.

Even in Greek mythology there is the notion that Icarus ascended on some form of kite. The legend, which tells of his ill-fated flight on wings made from wax and feathers, and his untimely descent into the waters of the Aegean Sea, could easily be describing a primitive man-carrying device.

Below: *A fanciful depiction of Icarus' failed attempt to fly with wings of wax and feathers.*

EGYPTIAN EVIDENCE

Myth often gives rise to speculation about the truth on which it may be founded. The Elephantine Papyrus, made in Egypt in around 500 B.C., is a hieroglyphic account of a legendary palace being constructed in the sky, between Heaven and Earth. It tells of eagles carrying building materials aloft; an unlikely event in itself, but research into these images has unfolded some remarkable possibilities.

Archaeologists found that the imagery of the Elephantine Papyrus bore similarity to much older stone carvings also located in Egypt. However, these

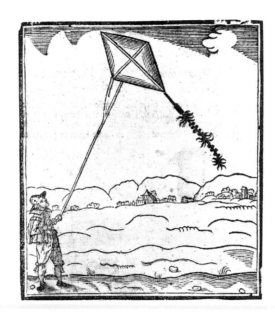

stone images clearly depict a group of people standing at ground level holding lines of twine or rope. A question arises: could they have been using large kites as a means of hoisting materials aloft? After all, this practice was developed during a later era in Japan. The eagles mentioned in the papyrus possibly amount to little more than poetic license taken by its author, who may not have been familiar with the concept of kites.

Further proof of an ancient Egyptian interest in flight can be found in the archives of Cairo Museum. The object in question is a highly stylized clay model of a bird which dates back to around 200 B.C. Bird forms in Egyptian art of this era are not unusual, but this one is distinguished by its maker's understanding of fundamental aerodynamics. At a glance, this bird could be mistaken for a twentieth-century model glider.

Left: *A seventeenth-century print depicting the notorious Fiery Drake.*

USE BY THE ROMANS

During the first century A.D., the Romans adopted hollow windsock banners which they termed Draci: the Latin for dragons. So named because of their fearsome adornment, they probably fell into Roman hands during a Middle Eastern conflict. Not only were these fitting standards to carry into battle, they also indicated wind direction, giving the Roman archers an advantage over enemy troops. Gradually, these windsocks evolved, unhitched from supporting poles to become kites, as illustrations in fourteenth-century manuscripts attest.

DEVELOPMENT IN EUROPE

By the early 1600s, the more conventional diamond-shaped kite had become popular in Europe. This was a direct descendant of similarly shaped kites that had long been popular in Malaysia. This style has endured to the present day, becoming widely recognized. Its familiar shape appears in A. A. Milne's stories of Winnie The Pooh. It was also immortalized as the sort of kite which carried Mary Poppins over the roof tops of London.

Kites entered Europe via the silk trade routes from the Orient to become an established part of the culture.

Perhaps the most dangerous toy of its time was the Fiery Drake, which appeared during the seventeenth century, taking the form of a gunpowder-laden device that was ignited when aloft. The result was a rapid, vertical volley of firecrackers followed by a final flare of light as the entire kite exploded into flames. Such a scene was magnificently recalled by the writer, John Bates, who in 1634 described the method of construction: coat the linen sail of a kite with linseed oil and shellac, then make a tail from paper and firecrackers. For added awesomeness, sulfur, pitch, and wax could be painted onto the sail, and a "fiery" message dramatically displayed.

By the 1640s, these kites were hissing and crackling wrathful messages from God in far-flung missionary posts. And so it happened that kites also became vehicles for airborne advertising.

AIDS TO SCIENCE

In the mid-eighteenth century, scientists looked skyward and started to use kites to explore atmospheric phenomena. The first recorded experiment was conducted by a Scotsman named Alexander Wilson. In 1749 he made highly ingenious use of kites to lift a series of thermometers in order to measure the air temperature at various altitudes ranging up to 3,000ft (900m).

Three years later, in 1752, Benjamin Franklin attached a metal key to the string of his kite and flew it, somewhat perilously, in a thunderstorm, proving lightning to be a visible discharge of electricity. The innovative Franklin was also credited with the invention of an early form of body surfing when he harnessed the pulling power of a large kite to propel himself across a pond.

Left: *Since the 1870s, kites have been used to lift cameras for aerial photography.*

Right: *George Pocock's Char Volant traveled the English highway drawn by arch-top kites.*

TRANSPORTATION

This quest for an airborne means of traction was later to become the obsession of George Pocock, a schoolteacher from Bristol, in England. In 1826, Pocock patented his revolutionary invention, the Char Volant, a carriage towed by a number of English arch-top kites. This forerunner of the modern three-wheeled kite buggy was able to carry four passengers at speeds of up to 20 miles (32km) an hour. It posed a problem, however, for toll collectors as there was nothing in nineteenth-century English law that defined such a vehicle. Consequently, no road tax could be collected from Pocock, and for a time he was allowed to ride the English West Country highways for free.

Although restricted in its movement by the wind's strength and direction, the Char Volant could be steered by means of two or more control lines attached to the kites themselves. Not only had Pocock set the wheels of kite-powered transportation in motion, he had also planted vital seeds for the development of a later generation of aerobatic sport kites.

Recently, in the 1980s, a New Zealand-based kite designer, Peter Lynn, improved this form of traction with the invention of a combined steerable aerofoil kite and buggy system which can be used on a variety of terrains, including water and ice. Nowadays, buggy pilots using this system can travel at speeds of more than 50 miles (80km) per hour.

ONE OF PROFESSOR ALEXANDER GRAHAM BELL'S RECENT EXPERIMENTS WITH A KITE COMPOUNDED OF SMALL TETRAHEDRAL KITES.

Drawn by E. J. Meeker from a photograph.

Above left: *Alexander Graham Bell holding a miniature version of his tetrahedral kite.*

Above: *Bell's tetrahedral kite could be assembled in various configurations to produce different flight characteristics.*

Left: *French designer Maillot devised a lifting system similar to Baden-Powell's (see page 20). This print depicts a test flight with a heavy payload.*

INTO THE TWENTIETH CENTURY

The beginning of the twentieth century heralded a renaissance in kite design and technology as kites became the foundation upon which early aviation was to be based. One of the pioneers of "man-lifting" was B. F. S. Baden-Powell, brother of the founder of the Boy Scout movement. Baden-Powell was an officer in the Scots Guards regiment, and during his military career he developed a kite suited to low-level reconnaissance. His "Levitor" was a variation on the Japanese Rokkaku kite and, with its enormous 36-ft (11m) sail, could lift a man high enough to see over enemy lines. The Levitor won its place in history during peacetime, however, when in 1901 it was used by Marconi to carry a wireless receiving aerial to a height of 400ft (122m). The result was the first-ever transatlantic radio broadcast.

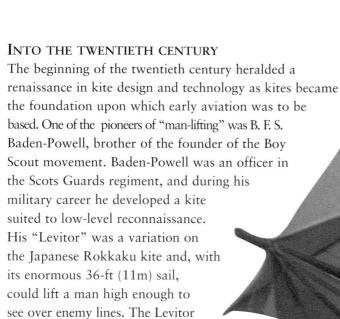

Above: An eager aviator takes a leap of faith in an attempt to cross a swimming pool by kite.

Above: One of Baden-Powell's creations is held aloft in preparation for takeoff.

One of the leading lights of modern aviation was Lawrence Hargrave, who from his home in New South Wales, Australia, developed ideas based on a simple two-cell box kite. Hargrave studied various wing shapes and introduced curved aerofoils into his designs for increased lift. His box kites, renowned for their stability, were used in meteorological forecasting during the first half of this century. The same inherent stability made Hargrave's kites ideal for man-lifting, and for that purpose he developed larger, rectangular box sails reminiscent of biplanes. The results of Hargrave's labor clearly had an enormous impact on later aircraft and kite design.

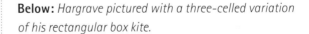

Above: *Lawrence Hargrave and James Swaine conduct an experiment to determine the pulling power of a man-lifting kite.*

Below: *Hargrave pictured with a three-celled variation of his rectangular box kite.*

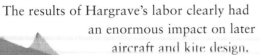

CODY THE PIONEER

Probably the most eccentric and daring pioneer of kite-powered man-lifting techniques was Samuel Franklin Cody. A Texan by birth, Cody settled in England during 1890 following a highly animated career as a cattle rancher and gold prospector. He was not, however, seeking early retirement and soon immersed himself in the quest for manned flight.

Cody's first kite was a version of Hargrave's box designs, with the addition of a large pair of scalloped wings extending out from the kite's main structure. He patented this design in 1901, and later the same year demonstrated it to the British war office, which immediately recognized its military potential as a man-lifting device.

During the period before the advent of military aviation, the available means of determining distant enemy movement was somewhat limited. A hazardously vulnerable device had been introduced in the 1860s at the time of the American Civil War. Taking the form of a tethered, hydrogen-filled balloon made of rubberized silk, this early spy craft had the capacity to lift its passenger a giddying 1,500 feet above the lines of battle, but was rendered cumbersome by a mass of accompanying equipment. A simpler reconnaissance system was needed, and Cody's seemed to be the obvious choice.

When flown in tandem, Cody's kites had colossal pulling power and were easily capable of lifting their creator to a height of 800ft (244m). Even so, during one demonstration of his apparatus to the Royal Navy, Cody, dressed in full Texan regalia, was forced to eject himself from the basket in which he was suspended beneath the kite rig, and plummeted

Left: *Samuel Franklin Cody, one of the twentieth century's kite heroes. Cody was also an avid aviationist.*

Below: *Through flamboyant feats of daring, Cody became a household name. His kite design is celebrated here on a cigarette card.*

30ft (9m) into the icy water below. In another famous episode, Cody crossed the English Channel in a small boat towed by his kites, but shortly after beginning the voyage in France he was becalmed and arrived, exhausted, in Dover some thirteen hours later.

Cody's celebrated aviation career ended on August 7, 1913, when, during a test flight, his "water plane" crashed to earth, killing both himself and his passenger. The legend lived on, however, and Cody's kites are much sought by worldwide collectors of kite and aviation artefacts.

Above: A battalion of Royal Engineers prepares a Cody man-lifter for use in low-level reconnaissance.

Right: A battleship plows its course upwind towing a series of Cody man-lifters.

Left: Collapsing man-lifters being rescued from stormy seas during Royal Navy reconnaissance trials in Portsmouth harbor in England.

LATER DEVELOPMENTS

During World War II, a US naval commander, Paul Garber, hit upon the idea of using kites as practice targets. To suit this purpose, he designed a 7-ft (2.1m)-tall diamond kite with a twin bridle that could be steered around in the sky. Decorated with the outline of an enemy plane, Garber's kite was the ultimate test of any gunner's skill.

Yet again, kites played a vital role in aeronautical research when in 1948 an American engineer, Francis Rogallo, patented the flexible delta wing. Although it was conceived as a safe means of recovering rocket boosters during the infancy of the US space program, this kite later formed the basis for hang-gliders.

A NEW GENERATION

A totally new form of kite emerged in 1963 when Domina Jalbert, using his knowledge of parachute design, came up with the parafoil. Based on a curved aerofoil wing shape, Jalbert's kite was revolutionary in its ability to fly without the need for any rigid supporting structure. Not only did this make for a much lighter and more efficient kite, it also simplified storage and transportation. Parafoils are able to lift considerable payloads, so it is not surprising that they are the most popular choice for archaeologists who use aerial photography on field studies of ancient sites.

By the beginning of the 1970s, kite design was booming. Aided by the wider availability of lightweight materials such as ripstop nylon, fiberglass, and carbon fiber, a whole new generation of kites came into being. Among these were the flexifoil power kite, designed by Andrew Jones and Ray Merry; the Peter Powell Diamond Stunter, and the Swept-wing or Delta Stunter.

Naturally, the emergence of so many new steerable kites has given rise to an international competition circuit, providing a forum for stunt pilots to show off their talents. Competitors are judged in both precision maneuvers and choreographed ballet routines. Undoubtedly the most spectacular

Below: *Three flexifoils flown in tandem. This classic design has barely changed since its invention in the 1970s and remains one of the most popular kite forms today.*

Above: *This Jalbert Parafoil bears the distinctive graphic style of Danish kite maker Jürgen Möllerhansen.*

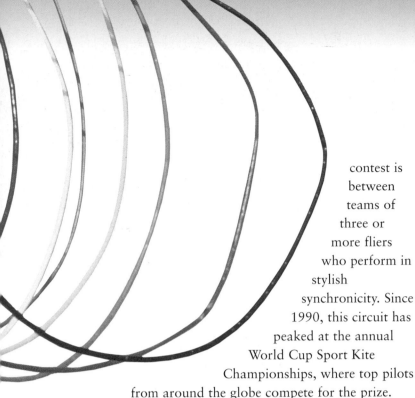

contest is between teams of three or more fliers who perform in stylish synchronicity. Since 1990, this circuit has peaked at the annual World Cup Sport Kite Championships, where top pilots from around the globe compete for the prize.

It was during the mid 1980s that the evolution of the swept-wing sport kite began to accelerate. California kite enthusiasts Don and Pat Tabor had recently established Top Of The Line, a sport-kite manufacturing company based in San Diego. One of their earliest designs, the Hawaiian Team Kite, flew with such grace and precision that it inspired Don Tabor to form a kite aerial-display team with fellow enthusiasts Ron Reich, Eric Streed, and Pam Kirk. Also named Top of The Line, this team began to travel the globe inspiring hundreds of fliers to follow suit.

Taking a dramatic and often emotive musical score, Ron Reich, the team's choreographer, would devise a complex and visually stunning routine. Reich's innovative choreographic style incorporated kaleidoscopic bursts, precise transitional geometric forms, and delicate weaves. Then would follow months of practice in diverse wind conditions as the team honed their skills in preparation for a long season of public displays and competitions.

By the late 1980s, new teams had emerged from all over the world with such names as The Blitz, Chicago Fire, High Performance, The Ballet Tutus, Up Against The Wall, and Flashback. Solo flyers, too, with conspicuous talents, have emerged over the past decade, and aided by a highly skilled international panel of judges, this esthetic sport is still growing apace.

With all these developments, spread over thousands of years, it is clear that the future of kite flying and design is as boundless as human imagination and ingenuity.

Left: *The Peter Powell Diamond Stunter combined tradition with new technology to take the kite world by storm during the 1970s. Equipped with a tough fiberglass frame, it easily withstood the rigors of flight at the hands of any novice.*

Below: *Formed in 1988, The Decorators is one of the world's longest-established kite display teams. Seen here, flying Revolutions customized by Jürgen Möllerhansen, are (from left to right) Jacob Twyford, Damon Meheux, Felix Mottram, Johnny Claffey, Romney Johnstone, and Andy Preston.*

Types of kite

A broad diversity of kites exists
throughout the globe, ranging
from small, simple constructions
to vast flying sculptures. This
chapter takes a look at twenty
different single-line and steerable
kites from around the world,
describing their origins and
how they perform.

A kite's anatomy

The four kites shown on pages 28–31 have among them most of the features to be found in the kites illustrated in this chapter.

Swept-wing sport kite

This type of dual-line steerable kite usually features a lightweight carbon-fiber frame and ripstop nylon sail.

Swept-wing sport kites normally range in wingspan from 3 to 8ft (1–2.4m), although larger models are available in most specialist kite shops.

As a general rule, the larger the sail area a kite has, the less wind it will require to fly, although this rule is guided by the weight of materials used in the kite's construction.

Nose – reinforced with tough webbing

Spine located in top and bottom pockets at the rear of the sail

Top spreader spar

Three-legged bridle. This can be adjusted to alter the kite's angle of attack by moving the nose forward in a strong wind or backward in a light wind.

Dacron reinforcement

Leading edge reinforced by a Dacron sleeve which houses the leading-edge spars

Sail made from panels of lightweight ripstop nylon

Trailing edge (a loose trailing edge will vibrate when the kite is flown and produce a rasping sound)

T Connector joining bottom spreaders and connecting them to the spine

Arrow nock at tail tip to locate sail-tensioning bungee cord

Pilot kite

Also known as the French Signal because of its resemblance to much larger kites once used by the French navy in rescue operations, the Pilot is an easily constructed triangular-celled box kite. A pair of lateral wings give this kite additional lift and stability so it can, with a little adjustment to the towing point, fly in light, as well as moderate or stronger winds.

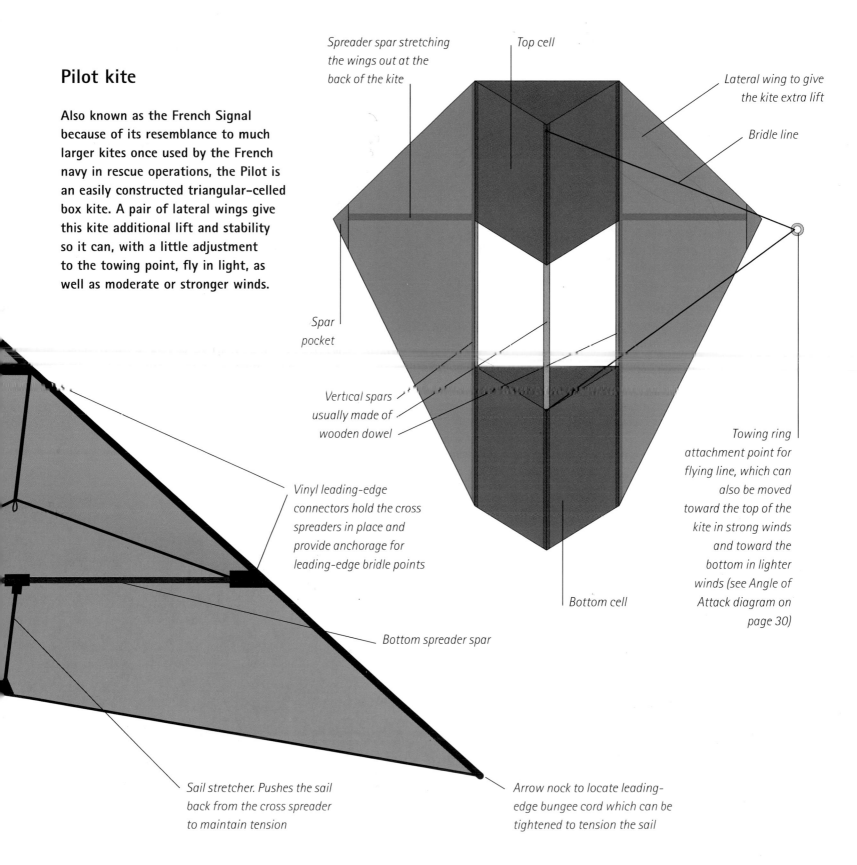

Spreader spar stretching the wings out at the back of the kite

Top cell

Lateral wing to give the kite extra lift

Bridle line

Spar pocket

Vertical spars usually made of wooden dowel

Towing ring attachment point for flying line, which can also be moved toward the top of the kite in strong winds and toward the bottom in lighter winds (see Angle of Attack diagram on page 30)

Vinyl leading-edge connectors hold the cross spreaders in place and provide anchorage for leading-edge bridle points

Bottom cell

Bottom spreader spar

Sail stretcher. Pushes the sail back from the cross spreader to maintain tension

Arrow nock to locate leading-edge bungee cord which can be tightened to tension the sail

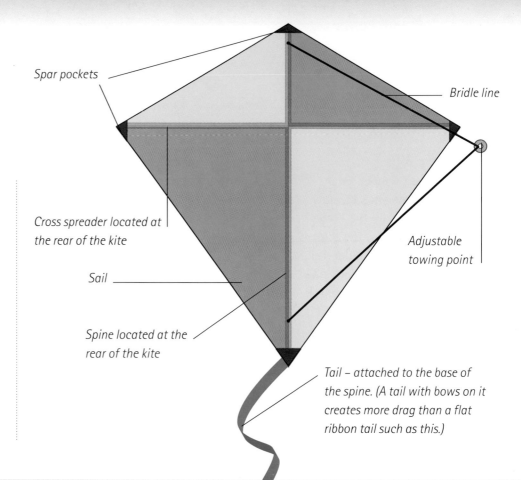

Spar pockets

Bridle line

Malay kite

The familiar diamond-shaped Malay is virtually an icon among kites. Although it has been around for centuries, this simple, elegant design is still as popular among die-hard hobbyists as it is among novice fliers. Like the Pilot kite, a Malay can be flown in a variety of wind speeds, though stronger winds may necessitate a longer or heavier tail to enhance the kite's stability. If you would like to try your hand at making a Malay, follow the instructions on pages 96–99.

Cross spreader located at the rear of the kite

Sail

Adjustable towing point

Spine located at the rear of the kite

Tail – attached to the base of the spine. (A tail with bows on it creates more drag than a flat ribbon tail such as this.)

Angle of Attack

The term Angle of Attack refers to the angle of the face of a kite in relation to the wind. This can be adjusted by altering the position of the towing point on the kite's bridle:

In a strong wind the towing point should be moved up the bridle, causing the nose of the kite to tilt forward into the wind so that pressure on the sail is reduced. This adjustment will help to stabilize the kite, at the same time reducing its pulling power.

Conversely, in a light wind, the towing point should be moved down the bridle so that the kite faces more fully into the wind. Only fractional adjustments are required to achieve stability.

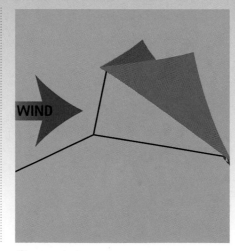

Strong wind

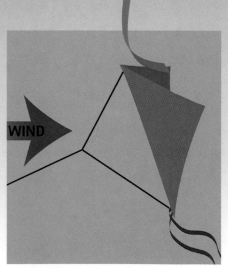

Light wind

Parafoil

Born in the early 1960s to aeronautical engineer Domina Jalbert, this sparless kite makes ingenious use of the wind to sustain its shape. Parafoils range in scale from little pocket-sized kites to gigantic canopies capable of bearing a fairly hefty person aloft. The parafoil illustrated here is a simple manifestation of the form. Some of the larger kites of this type have numerous cells and several rows of keels yielding multiple bridles.

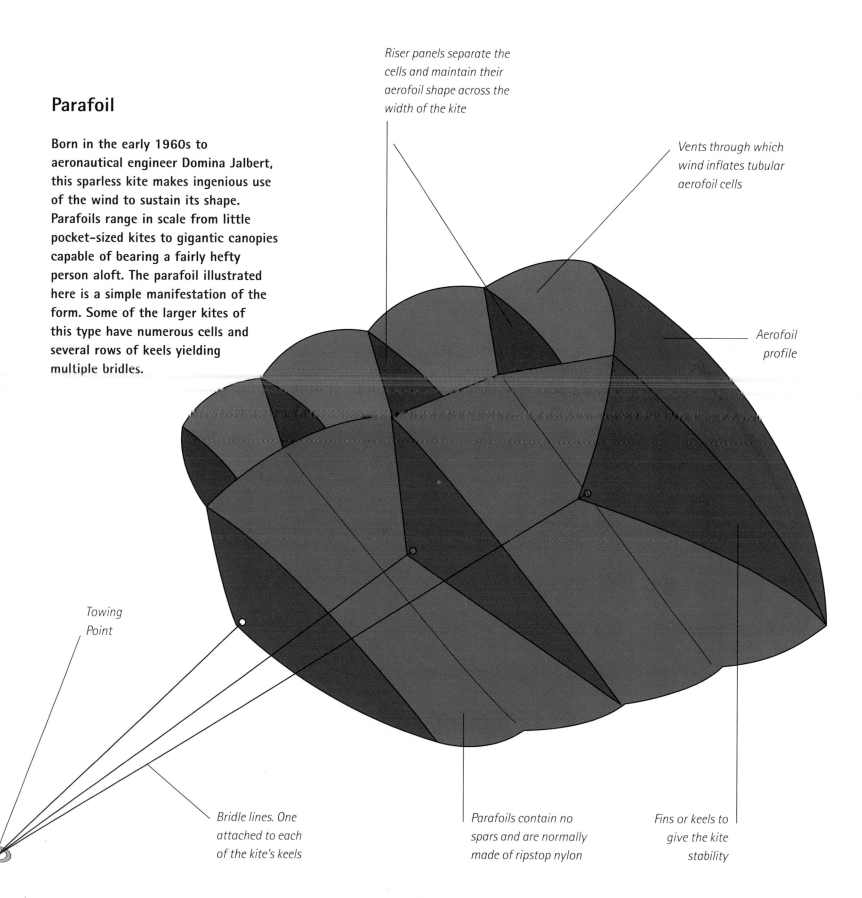

Riser panels separate the cells and maintain their aerofoil shape across the width of the kite

Vents through which wind inflates tubular aerofoil cells

Aerofoil profile

Towing Point

Bridle lines. One attached to each of the kite's keels

Parafoils contain no spars and are normally made of ripstop nylon

Fins or keels to give the kite stability

Types of kite

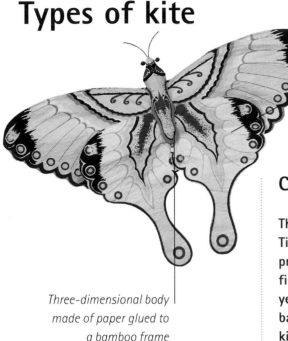

Four separate wings are pegged into holes in the body frame

Three-dimensional body made of paper glued to a bamboo frame

Chinese butterfly

This modern butterfly kite from Tianjin, near Beijing in eastern China, probably bears close similarity to the first Chinese kites made about 2,500 years ago. Constructed of paper and bamboo, this colorful hand-painted kite is one of the most basic types being manufactured in China today. It is not uncommon to find kites such as this for sale in many of the world's kite shops. Silk kites in the form of butterflies, birds, and centipedes are much sought, but a little more elusive outside China itself.

China is still the home of some of the world's greatest kite makers and hosts one of the largest and most diverse kite festivals in the world. Each spring since 1985, the city of Weifang has had its skies filled with kites from virtually every continent in an international celebration of wind and flight.

Maori bird

For centuries, this type of bird kite has been flown on the myriad islands throughout Oceania. The one depicted here was made in New Zealand during the mid-nineteenth century and currently resides in the archives of the Museum of Mankind in London, England. It has a wooden frame supporting a sail made from raupu vine leaves and is decorated with fragments of seashell and feathers. Representing a male bird, this kite would normally play a role in fertility rites.

Similar kites, also made of the raupu vine or of palm leaves, are still flown in parts of Polynesia by fishermen who use them as an aid to the long-range casting of their fishing lines.

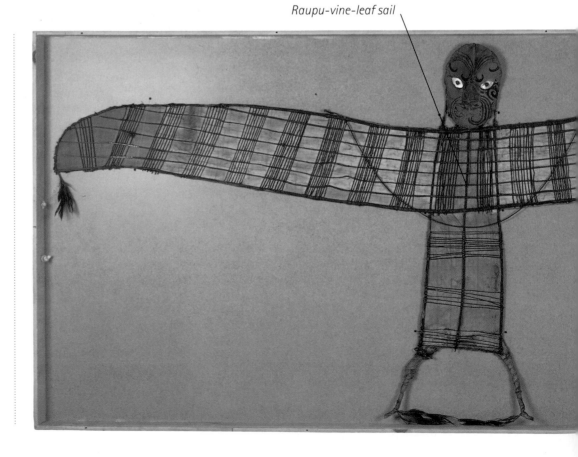

Raupu-vine-leaf sail

Balinese bird

The tiny Indonesian island of Bali has a long tradition of kite flying. Originally made from bamboo and silk, Balinese bird kites have endured to become symbols of beauty and serenity as they flock high on ocean breezes. In recent years, a rapidly growing tourist industry has increased the demand for these kites massively, and nowadays, although still hand finished, they are predominantly made of nylon.

During the 1970s, as windsurfing gathered popularity, a new source of kite-making material could suddenly be found littering Bali's beaches. Discarded windsurfer sails were quickly recycled by local entrepreneurs to re-enter the tourist market as kites, thereby perpetuating a union with the wind.

Three-dimensional body and head covered with fabric feathers

Bamboo frame

Bamboo wing spars

Indian fighting

Kites are a significant part of the culture of India. In fact, kite fighting is high on India's list of national sports and small paper fighters, like those pictured here, can often be seen jostling in the skies above Indian cities, towns, and villages. In the middle of large urban centers, kites are usually flown from rooftops, sometimes resulting in mishap when an over-zealous pilot misses his footing and drops into the street below.

Made of tissue paper and weighing very little, Indian fighters are among the lightest and most agile kites. The secret of their agility is a bowed cross spar made of split bamboo which has been tapered at each end to increase its flexibility.

The effect is quite simple. As wind strikes the surface of the kite, its pressure forces the cross spreader to bow backward. This forms the kite into a dihedral angle, making it stable and causing it to move in the direction that its tip is pointing. Rapidly playing out line reduces the pressure on the face of the kite; the cross spar straightens, and the kite becomes unstable. At this point it will spin, and a well-timed tug on the line will send it moving in a direction of the pilot's choice.

Perhaps because of their proliferation on such a vast continent, these tiny kites have become familiar the world over. Their poetic simplicity seems to touch the consciousness of every traveler to India.

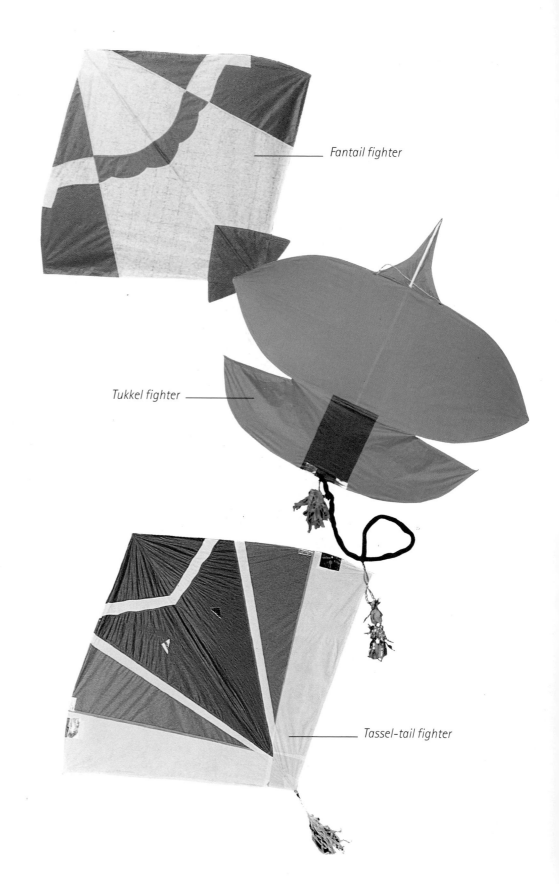

Fantail fighter

Tukkel fighter

Tassel-tail fighter

Sanjo Rokkaku

This popular form of fighting kite has its origins in Japan. Traditional Rokkakus are made of fibrous paper and decorated with powerfully expressive portraits depicting characters from Japanese history. Fearsome livid Samurai warriors painted with vivacious brush strokes are typical of Rokkaku imagery.

Rokkaku battles are a popular feature of many kite festivals as teams of skilled fliers pit their wits against each other in a frantic bid to cut their opponent's strings or tip each others' kites out of the sky. The last remaining airborne kite is the winner.

Nowadays, because of their international appeal among a growing combatant fraternity, Rokkakus are customized and adorned in the manner of formula-one racing cars. Ripstop nylon sails provide durability in battle, and distinguishing graphics announce the sponsors and handling team of each kite.

Adjustable six-legged bridle

This contemporary Rokkaku made by Mick Jennison bears the Japanese crane symbol

Wau Bulan

The Wau Bulan is so named because of the low, resonant sound that it makes as it flies: "wau-wau-wau." This note is sustained when a tape, tightly stretched across a bamboo bow attached to the frame, vibrates in the wind. In Malaysia, the home of the Wau Bulan, music is often a feature of kites, many of which are fitted with hummers playing in the manner of simple aeolian (wind) harps.

The highly decorative kite depicted here was probably intended for ceremonial purposes. Its sail is adorned with a traditional pattern of foliage. Some of the more elaborate Wau Bulan sails are decorated with intricate collages of gold paper and stand over 7ft (2.1m) high. Smaller kites of this distinctive shape, made of plain paper, are more commonly flown throughout Malaysia.

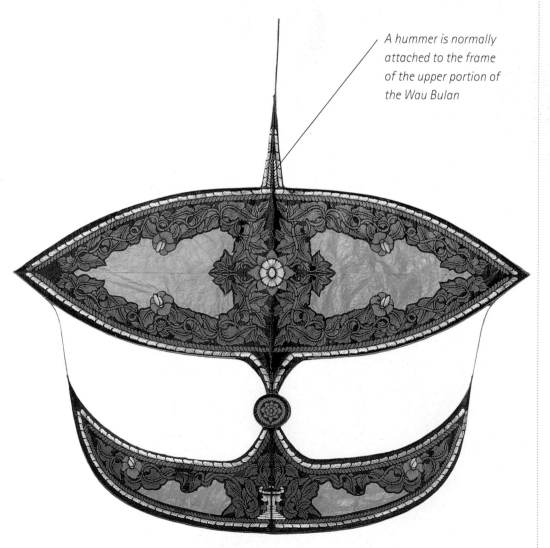

A hummer is normally attached to the frame of the upper portion of the Wau Bulan

Barroletta

This magnificent kite has been adopted into Guatemalan Indian culture as a symbol of the sun, which lay at the very heart of ancient Mayan culture. Its frame is a cart-wheel-like construction of bamboo, lashed together with twine, and its sail is formed of thousands of tiny pieces of colored tissue paper joined with paste.

These kites are made in the small hillside village of Santiago Sacatepequez, to be flown on November 1, All Saints' Day. The setting for this festival is a graveyard, where each year the peace is broken in a rush of aerial mayhem as the locals launch their creations. It is said that the annual harvest depends on the successful flight of these prophetic Barrolettas, but fly or fall, at the end of the day each kite is stripped from its frame and burned.

No one seems to know exactly how this ritual originated, though local folklore offers a variety of explanations. One version tells of a village shaman who advised locals that evil spirits could be driven from the graveyard by the sound of rustling paper over the graves. Another suggests that the kites evoke heavenly bodies, their tails symbolizing ladders by which the souls of the dead might reach the heavens.

Though it seems plausible that these kites found their way into Guatemala via Spanish trading routes through the Caribbean, the facts of their genesis have yet to be determined.

Sail patterns vary, often symbolizing historic events or tribal distinctions

Bamboo frame

Malay

This is a variation on one of Malaysia's oldest and best-known kites. Diamond kites like this have been flown in Europe since the early seventeenth century, and because of their simplicity, they are popular among beginners.

The spars of a Malay are usually made of wooden dowel, and the sail, though once made of cotton, is nowadays more likely to be ripstop nylon. In fact, most modern kites are made of ripstop because it weighs very little and has a low porosity, preventing too much air from passing through the sail itself.

Tails are often attached to Malays as stabilizers, though the vertical spine of the kite forms a keel in flight which serves the same purpose.

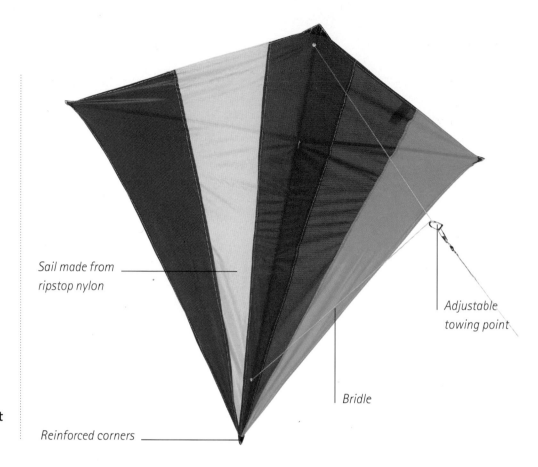

Sail made from ripstop nylon

Adjustable towing point

Bridle

Reinforced corners

Pipa

This small paper kite is the sort that Brazilian children make and fly to pass the time or earn some spending money. Also flown as a fighting kite, its stability can be modified by adding to or subtracting from the tail. A Pipa flown without its tail will have a tendency to rock from side to side.

The wood or bamboo frame is bound together with a long piece of twine. This twine is also wound right around the outer tips of the spars, giving them some extra support and strengthening the edges of the sail.

A tissue-paper sail is folded over this twine perimeter and held in place with glue. Each kite is finished with the addition of a long tail, cut from surplus paper.

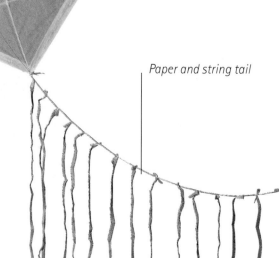

String perimeter

Paper and string tail

Winged box

Box kites are often associated with stronger winds, but the wings protruding from this one give it extra lift, allowing it to fly in a wind of as little as 8 miles (13km) an hour. Derived from the original Hargrave Box, this type of kite has broad appeal because of its reliable stability.

Large box kites of similar construction have been used to lift objects such as cameras or meteorological equipment. Basic two-celled box kites even played a role in World War II as radio-aerial hoists. Known as Gibson Girls, these bright yellow kites were an essential part of any airman's sea rescue kit as an aid to broadcasting distress signals.

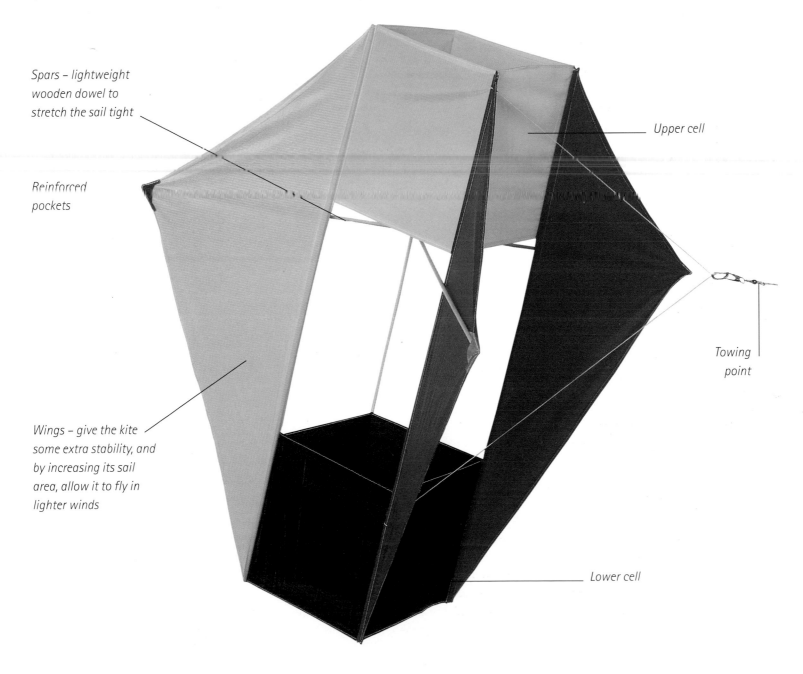

Spars – lightweight wooden dowel to stretch the sail tight

Reinforced pockets

Upper cell

Towing point

Wings – give the kite some extra stability, and by increasing its sail area, allow it to fly in lighter winds

Lower cell

Sled

This simple kite shape was conceived in 1950 by American designer W. M. Allison. Having no cross-bracing, it relies on the wind to form its curved shape in flight. Sleds prefer moderate, steady breezes, but the addition of a looped tail will help to prevent the kite from folding in on itself should the wind fluctuate.

These kites are ideal for workshops and classroom projects as they can easily be constructed from plastic sheeting, garden stakes, and tape. Some sleds have vents in their sails which, apart from adding decoration, serve to take some pressure off the surface in strong winds.

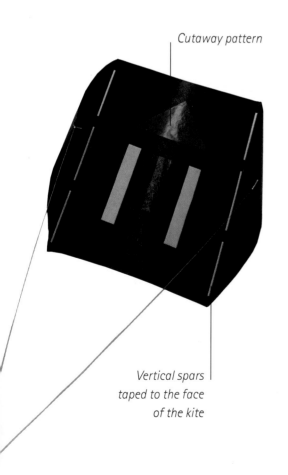

Cutaway pattern

*Vertical spars
taped to the face
of the kite*

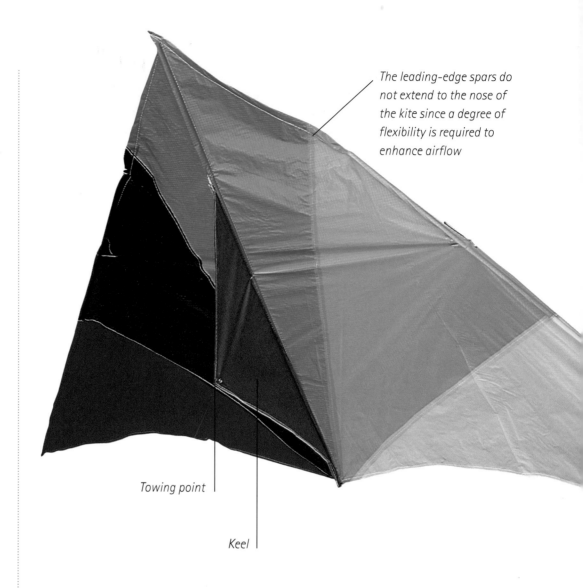

*The leading-edge spars do
not extend to the nose of
the kite since a degree of
flexibility is required to
enhance airflow*

Towing point

Keel

Delta

Delta kites evolved from Francis Rogallo's flexible wing kite of the 1940s. They are among the easiest kites in the world to fly and, because of their high angle of flight, can be flown in less than average wind. Once aloft, all they need to stay airborne are rising currents of hot air, known as thermals.

The presence of a keel, to which the flying line is attached, makes this kite stable throughout a wide range of wind speeds. Some Deltas have double skinned, or "balloon," keels, which serve as air brakes by giving added resistance to the wind, thereby stopping the kite from flying too far overhead and stalling. Others sport fringed trailing edges which create drag in the manner of a tail. This increases their stability in stronger winds.

Parafoil

Invented by Domina Jalbert, Parafoils have much in common with modern steerable parachutes. Having no rigid frame, they rely on a constant flow of air to keep their aerofoil cells inflated. This effect can be enhanced by means of holes cut into the internal ribs or risers which divide one cell from another across the width of the kite. The bridle lines of a Parafoil are attached to each of a series of keels, or fins, which protrude from the kite's belly. These fins act as stabilizers, limiting any sideways motion.

Because of their inherent stability, Parafoils are often used to lift cameras as an economical way of obtaining aerial photographs. Even video equipment can be lifted this way to produce dizzying and exciting footage.

Keels *Air intake* *Multiple bridle*

Lester's legs

Perhaps the strangest aerial phenomenon is this kite in the form of a gigantic, disembodied biped which can be seen kicking and dancing in the skies at kite festivals all over the world. This is the brainchild of designer Martin Lester and belongs to his bizarre flying menagerie which, aptly, includes the upper portion of a waving man.

The true cunning of these kites lies in their ability to imitate the movement of real, human limbs – an effect which is produced by the skillful juxtaposition of one ripstop panel with another. Ranging in length from 9 to 62ft (2.7–19m), the Legs can exert a massive pull which renders them as exhilarating to fly as they are surreal to observe.

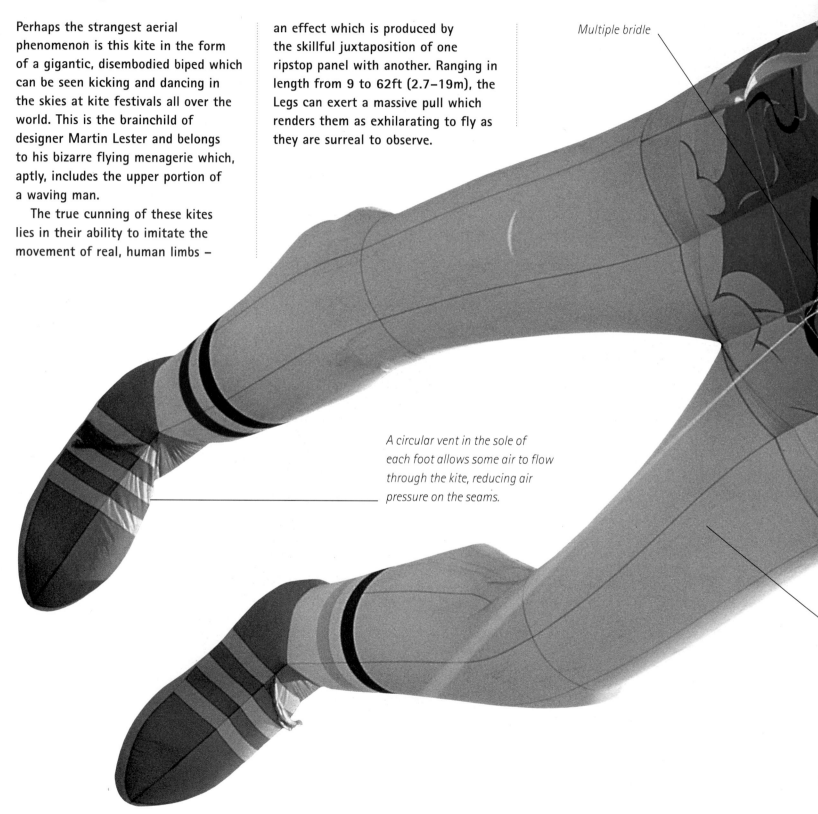

Multiple bridle

A circular vent in the sole of each foot allows some air to flow through the kite, reducing air pressure on the seams.

Diamond stunter (Blazer)

Air intake

This diamond-shaped stunt kite has a twin bridle to which a pair of flying lines are attached. This means it can be steered to the left or right by pulling the corresponding control line. When, for example, the pilot continues to pull on the right-hand line, the kite will keep turning in that direction, completing a full circle. Conversely, a pull on the left-hand line will cause the kite to change direction. Like the Indian fighter, any dual-control stunt kite will always travel in the direction that its tip or nose is pointing.

The speed of this kite is regulated by a long tubular tail which streams out behind it, describing loops, turns, and dives. A strong, flexible fiberglass frame helps to absorb the force of impact in the event of a crash, making the Blazer an ideal novice stunter.

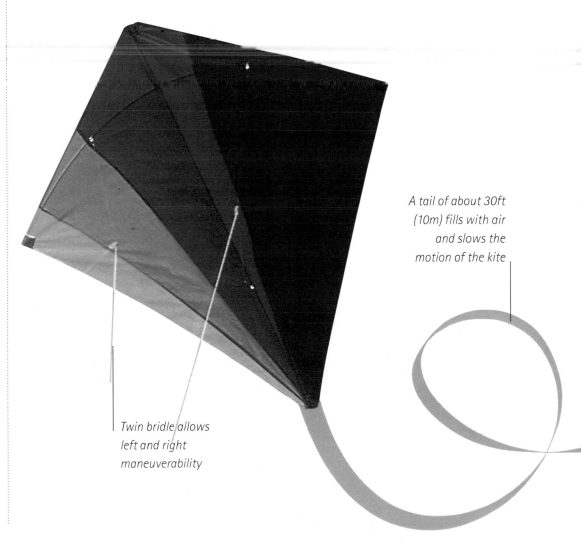

Keels giving lateral stability

The overall shape of this kite is based on a flowform Parafoil, though its construction and resulting dynamics are more complex

Twin bridle allows left and right maneuverability

A tail of about 30ft (10m) fills with air and slows the motion of the kite

Swept-wing stunter (Sandpiper)

The Sandpiper is a state-of-the-art swept-wing sport kite. It belongs to the recent generation of high-performance, dual-control kites favored by pilots on the growing competition circuit. Designed by Chris Matheson, one of Europe's leading sport-kite pilots, Sandpipers are built to perform diverse maneuvers ranging from tight, angular turns to smooth, fluid axle spins.

A frame of lightweight carbon-fiber rods and a cambered, ripstop nylon sail enhance the aerodynamic efficiency of the Sandpiper. Although capable of flying in as little as 4 miles (6.5km) an hour of wind in its standard format, the Ultra Light Sandpiper can be flown in barely tangible air currents. In fact, it was with this kite at the London Docklands Arena, in 1995, that Matheson established an indoor kite-flying world record of two hours and two minutes.

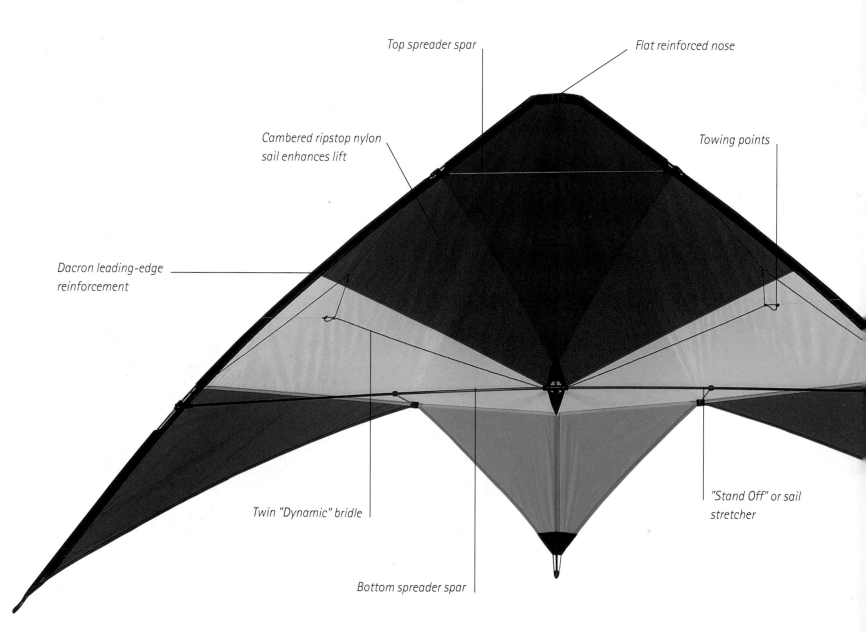

Top spreader spar

Flat reinforced nose

Cambered ripstop nylon
sail enhances lift

Towing points

Dacron leading-edge
reinforcement

"Stand Off" or sail
stretcher

Twin "Dynamic" bridle

Bottom spreader spar

44

Speed runner

This kite is similar in appearance to a paraglider, but with a wing span of 8ft (2.4m), it is much smaller. Its designer, Jim Rowlands, has based its construction on an elliptical plan form with a multiple bridle system. The bridle lines are attached to each alternate aerofoil cell over the front 20 percent of the canopy.

Having considerable pull for their size, Speed Runners fall into the power-kite category and, in strong winds, can tax the strength of even the toughest pilot. A larger version, known as the Vector, can be used for buggy racing.

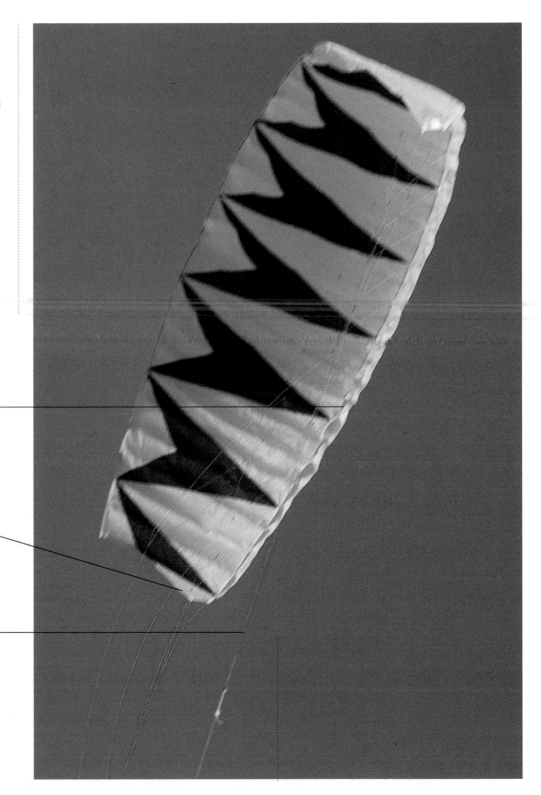

Air intake

Wingtip keel

Multiple bridle

Flexifoil

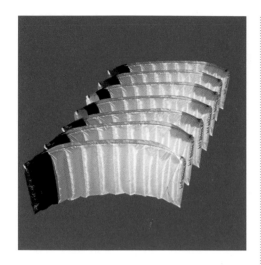

Above: *A stack of six flexifoils carves through the air with graceful ease but muscle testing power.*

Designed in the 1970s by Andrew Jones and Ray Merry, the Flexifoil is still at the forefront of power kite technology. Ranging in span from 4 to 12ft (1.2–3.6m), these kites can be stacked together in tandem to produce an awesome force. For this reason, they are widely used in traction kiting where kites are made to pull boats, buggies, or skis. Flexifoils are world record holders in two areas: first for their ability to travel at speeds of up to 112 miles (180km) an hour; and second for the sport-kite stacking record of 208 Flexifoils, established in 1993.

The Flexifoil is constructed of a series of aerofoil pockets with a mesh vent at the leading edge. As wind rushes through this vent, the ripstop canopy inflates and the kite lifts off. A pair of control lines are attached, one at each end of a tapered spar which runs the length of the kite's leading edge; this flexes to form a curve as the kite takes off.

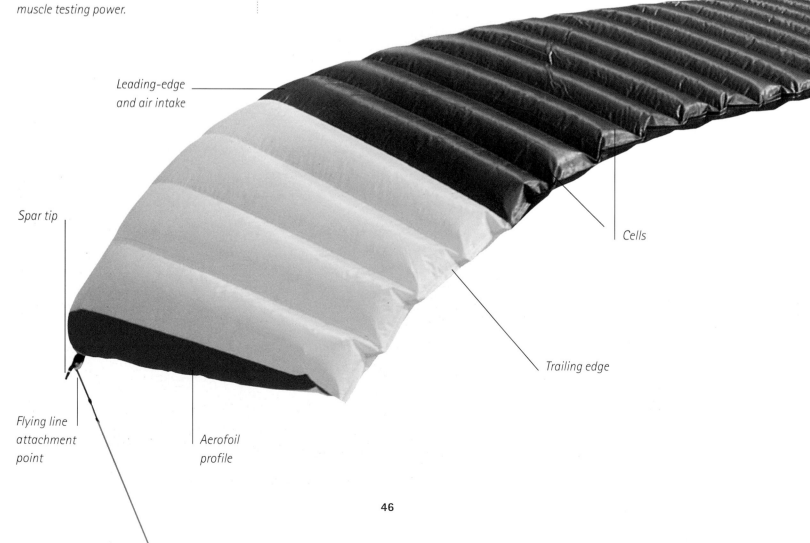

Leading-edge and air intake

Spar tip

Cells

Trailing edge

Flying line attachment point

Aerofoil profile

Left and below: *The force of a Flexifoil stack can be harnessed to propel water or land buggies. These kite-powered vehicles, originally developed by Peter Lynn, are steered by the riders' feet. The speeds at which these buggies will travel is affected by the force of the wind and the scale of kites used.*

Revolution

Originally known as the Neos Omega, this quad-line kite took the world by storm in the late 1980s. The Revolution was the outcome of a quest for a truly innovative aerodyne led by the California-based Hadziki brothers. Like dual-line kites, Revolutions can travel forward and be made to turn left or right. The genius of this kite, however, lies in its additional ability to fly backward, sideways, rotate on its central axis, or stop dead – whatever the wind speed.

The kite is controlled by means of two curved, tubular alloy handles to which flying lines are attached top and bottom. By tilting these handles backward and forward, a pilot can maneuver the Revolution with pinpoint accuracy.

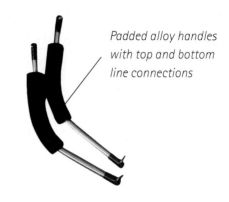

Padded alloy handles with top and bottom line connections

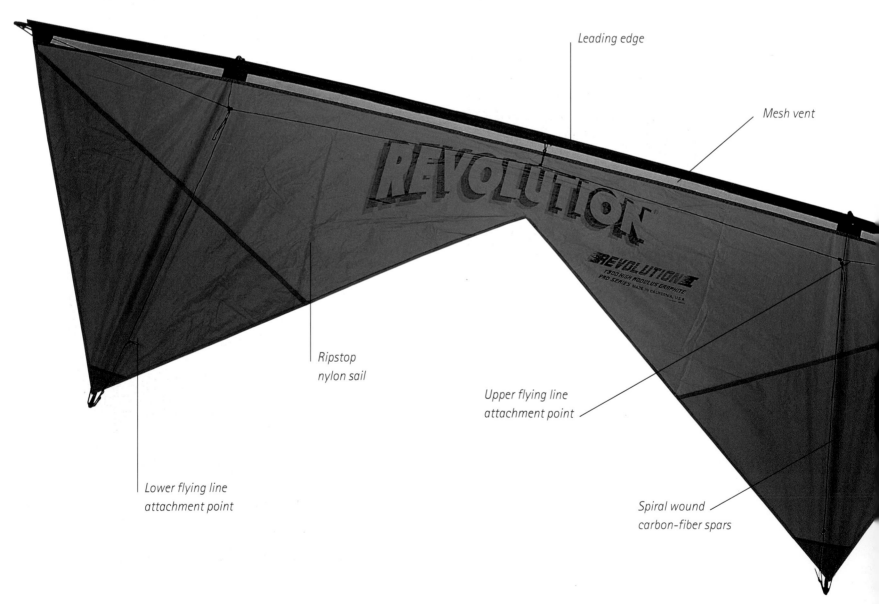

Leading edge

Mesh vent

Ripstop nylon sail

Upper flying line attachment point

Lower flying line attachment point

Spiral wound carbon-fiber spars

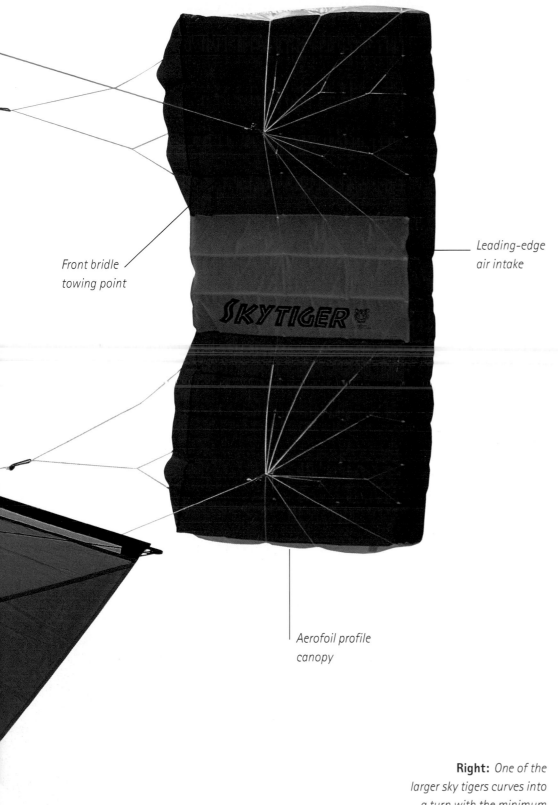

*Front bridle
towing point*

*Leading-edge
air intake*

*Aerofoil profile
canopy*

Sky tiger

These kites combine the quad-line steering system with a Flexifoil-style canopy. The resulting kite has a power that can be tamed in an instant by tilting the control handles forward to throw the kite into a stall. Recovery is simply a matter of tilting the handles back again to reinflate the canopy.

Sky Tigers range in span from 6½ to 15ft (2–4.6m), the larger kites being a popular choice of equipment for buggy pilots or devotees of any form of traction kiting.

Right: *One of the larger sky tigers curves into a turn with the minimum of pilot effort.*

49

Learning to fly

Part of the universal appeal
of kites lies in the fact that they
need only wind and space to
perform. Anyone can learn to fly
a kite and experience the thrill of
playing with the force of the air.
This section provides a basic
introduction to the methods
of launching and flying six
different types of kite.

Flying equipment

The items of equipment shown on these pages are used with the variety of static line and steerable kites described in this chapter. Naturally, the flying equipment that you need will depend on your choice of kite and the condition of the wind.

Revolution quad-line handles

Padded straps are safer to use with large power kites as they will not dig into your wrists.

Leather gloves to protect your hands from string burns

Dark glasses with full UV protection

This type of ring reel is pointed flat surface toward the kite to release line and turned at a right angle to the pilot's body to stop the line from reeling out.

Two-handed spools like this one are used by Indian-fighter-kite fliers.

Individual kite bag

Quad-line winder with
restraining elastic collar

Dacron low-stretch
sport-kite line

The basic requirements for a kite-flying session are quite simply a kite, some string, a cylindrical object to use as a reel – and wind. If you become one of the growing number of enthusiasts, however, there is every chance that you will need a voluminous kite bag in which to carry your assortment of kites and related gadgets. A kite bag is a little like a golf bag in the sense that just as a golfer needs a variety of clubs for various strokes, so do some kite flyers need a number of kites to deal with changes in flying style or wind speed. These days, with the help of kite lights, well-equipped pilots could fly for a continuous twenty-four hours, but unlike a golfer, can indulge their hobby in the comfort of an average-sized living room by using a tiny featherweight kite which can be kept aloft on thermals.

Whatever your flying tastes may be, it is always a good idea to carry a basic repair kit with you, as even the most seasoned fliers are prone to accidents or equipment failure. The items that you are most likely to need are extra spars compatible with those in the kite, spare line, and a sleeving kit if you happen to be using a low-stretch sport line. It is also a good idea to pack some tape, just in case the rough end of a broken spar should puncture the kite's sail. These items won't add much to the weight of the kit, but they will insure against frustration and disappointment.

Standard-weight
webbing wrist straps
are more comfortable
and secure to use with
dual-line kites than
plastic handles.

Plastic ground
stake

Dual-line storage
winder

Heavy-duty kite bag with side pockets
for storing accessories

Choosing a flying site

An ideal flying site will be free of trees, buildings or other obstructions. Look for a wide open space with a surface of grass or sand, and avoid sharp rocks or thorny plants which might damage the kite when you land it.

If there are any trees or buildings in the area make sure that you set the kite up as far down wind of them as possible. This will help to ensure that the kite is not affected by turbulence.

Right: *Large objects in the path of the wind will disrupt its flow and cause a kite to spiral and dive out of control.*

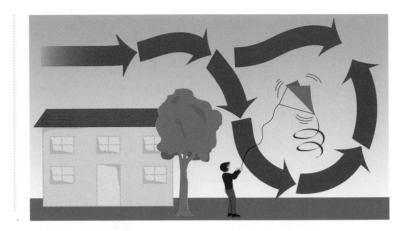

SAFETY TIPS

1 Never fly a kite near overhead power cables or in thunderstorms.

2 Avoid flying over the heads of other people or animals as this could cause them alarm or injury.

3 Don't fly near roads, railway lines or within 5km (3 miles) of any airport.

4 Check the maximum height limit in your country. (In the UK, this is 60m (200ft) as stated by the Civil Aviation Authority.)

5 It is a good idea to wear gloves if you are handling a single-line kite to avoid string burns.

6 Bear in mind that harmful ultraviolet rays can penetrate clouds, making a pair of sunglasses and a bottle of sunscreen a handy addition to your kite flying kit.

Gauging wind speed

This table gives a broad indication of wind strength. For more precise readings, wind-speed meters can be bought from kite shops or yacht chandlers.

Beaufort	Average km (miles) per hour	Effect on environment	Which kite?
1	2–5 (1.2–3)	Smoke just begins to move with the breeze	Ultra Light Delta
2	6–12 (3.7–7.5)	Leaves rustle slightly	Ultra Light or medium Delta
3	13–20 (8–12.5)	Small branches sway and smoke begins to move horizontally	Most kites fly well
4	21–30 (13–18.6)	Loose surface dust or sand is stirred and larger branches sway	Large kites will begin to pull
5	31–40 (19.3–25)	Surface waves begin to form on water	Good buggy conditions
6	41–50 (25.5–31)	Trees begin to bend with the force of the wind	Excellent for buggies, power kites, vented kites

Launching and flying a Delta

FLYING TIPS

LOCATION
Good choice of kite for an urban park due to its ability to gain height quickly and maintain a high angle of flight, thus avoiding turbulence from surrounding buildings and trees

NUMBER OF PEOPLE NEEDED
One

SUITABILITY FOR CHILDREN
Aged 8 years up, or younger with adult supervision

DEGREE OF DIFFICULTY
One of the easiest kites to learn with

ESSENTIAL ACCESSORIES
None

This small Delta kite has a wingspan of about 5ft (1.5m). Much larger Deltas need some physical strength to fly.

It is always important to select the right line strength for whichever kite you choose to fly. In this case, approximately 30- to 45-lb (15–20kg) test breaking strain will do.

A cylindrical reel will be perfect for the task of playing out or reeling in the line at speed, and a swivel clip will allow you to quickly secure the line to the kite. Swivels also prevent the line from tangling during flight.

1 *The line is attached to a point on the keel. Some Deltas have a choice of three points of attachment: one at the tip of the keel for moderate wind; one about ³/₈in (1cm) closer to the nose of the kite for stronger wind; and one about ³/₈in (1cm) closer to the rear of the kite for less wind.*

Cross-spreader pocket (the cross spreader lies at the rear of the kite)

Spine

Swivel clip attaching flying line to keel

BEAUFORT (1) (2) (3) (4) (5) (6)

High-wind attachment point

Right: *Close-up of keel*

Light-wind attachment point

Medium-wind attachment point

Leading edge

Keel

Trailing edge

2 *Stand with your back to the wind, holding the keel with one hand and the flying reel in the other. As wind billows the sail, release the kite and begin to play out the line.* ·

3 *It is important to keep a certain amount of tension in the line, but this should be slackened if the kite begins to spin or dive out of control. If the kite starts to sink, a gentle pull on the line will help it to rise again. Remember that the higher the kite, the stronger the wind, so always keep your eyes on the kite!*

4 *Landing the kite is simply a matter of reeling it back to your hands, keeping a lookout for any signs of instability as you do. Should the kite become unstable (say, spiral toward the ground), play the line out while walking toward the kite. When the kite is steady again, gently pull the line in again and continue to reel it in.*

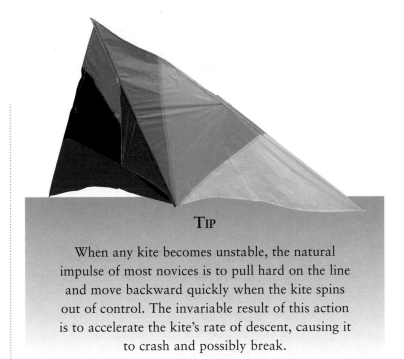

TIP

When any kite becomes unstable, the natural impulse of most novices is to pull hard on the line and move backward quickly when the kite spins out of control. The invariable result of this action is to accelerate the kite's rate of descent, causing it to crash and possibly break.

Launching and flying a winged box kite

FLYING TIPS

LOCATION
Can be flown in most suitable flying sites

NUMBER OF PEOPLE
Can be flown by one, but in higher winds two may be needed (see step 1)

SUITABILITY FOR CHILDREN
Aged 8 years up, or younger with adult supervision

DIFFICULTY
As simple as the Delta to fly, but needs a little wind

GENERAL ACCESSORIES
None

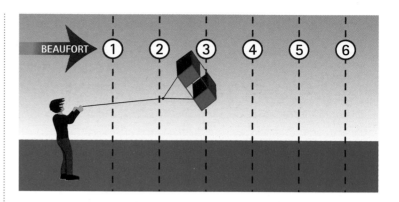

1 *Some kites, especially larger ones, are easier to launch with the help of a co-pilot. Having attached the flying line, (about 66–88lb [30–40kg] test), the co-pilot carries the kite downwind to a distance of about 30ft (10m) from the pilot and holds it up to the wind. When the pilot is ready, the kite is released and should immediately rise to assume its correct angle of flight. This technique, known as a "long launch," is particularly useful when the wind at ground level is too light to effect a hand launch.*

DROGUES

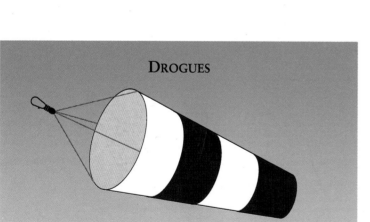

A drogue is like a small windsock, usually made of ripstop nylon and held open at its widest end by a narrow band of stiffening material such as fiberglass rod. When attached to the rear of the kite, it will have the same stabilizing effect as a tail. Drogues can also be attached to the flying line for a decorative effect. See how to make your own drogue on page 103.

2 *Box kites, like this one, usually require a wind strength of approximately 3 Beaufort, although they can be made stable in stronger wind by the addition of a drogue or wind sock.*

If the kite is large or tends to pull hard, it may be easier to land by placing the reel on the ground and hauling the line in hand over hand. It is essential to protect your hands with gloves if you are handling line this way.

Morgan Star Tumbling Box Kite

Although box kites are renowned for their ability to remain static in flight, moving only with the wind, this one is an exception to the rule. The Morgan Star is one of a variety of interactive box kites that are characterized by having a narrow side profile. Tumbling box kites can be maneuvered by the pilot, at will, in much the same way that an Indian fighter is maneuvered (see page 34). Once you have mastered the technique, you can challenge yourself to tumble the kite as close to the ground as you dare before correcting it.

This narrow-celled kite is bridled so that it flies at an angle tilting away from the pilot. When the kite is launched, it will assume a steady position on the wind, but if the pilot rapidly casts line off, the flying reel it will lose its stability and tumble backward toward the ground.

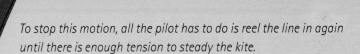

To stop this motion, all the pilot has to do is reel the line in again until there is enough tension to steady the kite.

Launching and flying a large Parafoil

FLYING TIPS

LOCATION
A wide open space, free of obstacles that may cause turbulence since parafoils need smooth and steady winds to inflate and fly

NUMBER OF PEOPLE
Two

CHILDREN
A kite of this size can pull strongly and may possibly lift a child off the ground (Smaller parafoils are suitable for children)

DIFFICULTY
Some flying experience with smaller kites is desirable

ESSENTIAL ACCESSORIES
Drogue, gloves

This is almost certainly a job for two people as a parafoil of this size can pull very hard indeed. A line strength of around 265-lb (120kg) test is being used here to make sure the kite won't break free if it is hit by a sudden gust of wind.

When selecting the appropriate line to fly a large kite, it is best to err on the side of caution and if necessary use a stronger line than recommended.

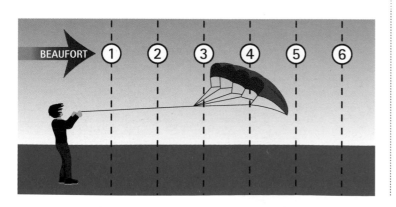

When flying a single-line kite of this size, it is absolutely essential to wear gloves. This will protect your hands from string burns.

1 *The pilot and co-pilot lay the kite out on the ground to prepare it for takeoff. After checking that all the shroud lines are free of tangles, they secure the flying line to the bridle loop. If any type of clip is used, it must have a breaking strain compatible with the flying line.*

Whereas smaller kites require only fishing swivels, a kite of this size will require a caribena connection. These are available from boat suppliers and outdoor-pursuit stores in a variety of strengths. A clip of this sort is not absolutely essential, however, as it is equally suitable to tie the flying line directly onto the bridle loop using a secure knot.

2 *When the kite is ready to launch, the co-pilot holds the canopy up, allowing wind to inflate each aerofoil cell. A long launch method is ideal for soft kites of this size as they need constant air pressure to stay inflated. Often a drogue tail is attached to the rear of the kite to produce extra drag. This streams behind the kite acting as a stabilizer.*

3 *As the kite is released, it will rise quickly. It is then the job of the co-pilot to help the pilot take the strain. Once aloft, a parafoil should remain steady in a moderate wind. If the wind drops suddenly, the canopy is in danger of collapsing, but can usually be reinflated by a steady pull on the line.*

4 *Because of its pulling power, a parafoil of this size will be easier to land by the "walk down" method. The co-pilot walks toward the kite pulling the line down hand over hand, with the pilot reeling in slack line behind him as she goes until the kite is safely on the ground.*
   This method can be aided by the use of a caribena clip attached to a strong wrist strap. The co-pilot simply hooks the clip over the flying line and walks toward the kite, pulling on the strap.

Launching and flying a swept-wing sport kite

Steerable kites are seldom flown on a line length of more than 50yd (50m). Longer lines, apart from slowing the responses of the kite, will make it difficult for the pilot to judge the kite's distance from obstacles.

The average wingspan of a swept-wing sport kite is about 8ft (2.4m), so the line strength should be approximately 150lb (70kg). Steerable kites use a different type of line from single-line kites. Commonly known as Spectra or Dyneema, this line is very tightly woven, making it much thinner than standard flying line to reduce drag when the kite is in motion. It also has very little stretch, so that the pilot's hand movements are immediately transmitted to the kite.

Most sport-kite pilots prefer to use wrist straps, as opposed to plastic handles, as they are more comfortable and secure.

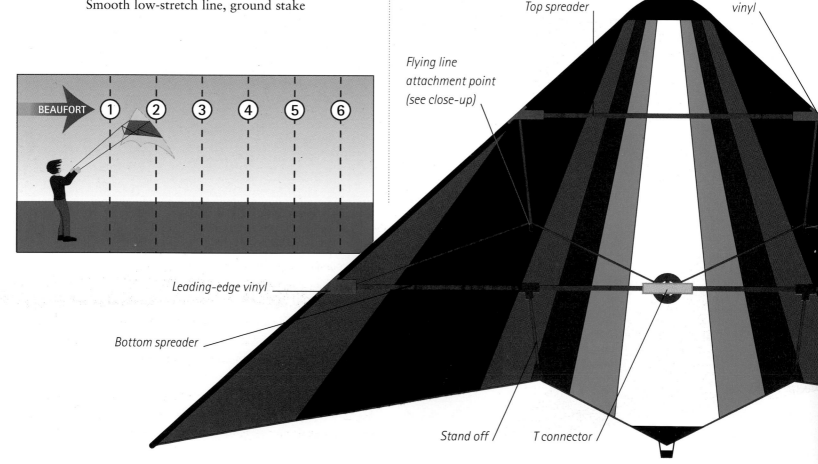

BEAUFORT ① ② ③ ④ ⑤ ⑥

Top spreader

Leading-edge vinyl

Flying line attachment point (see close-up)

Leading-edge vinyl

Bottom spreader

Stand off

T connector

Preparing for takeoff

1 *Assemble the kite, following the manufacturer's instructions. This will involve connecting a top spreader spar to vinyl tubes on the leading edge, two bottom spreader spars to the leading edge, and a T connector located on the spine. The sail is then stretched tight by connecting a pair of stand-offs to the bottom spreaders.*

Finally, check that the bridles are free of tangles before attaching the flying lines to the bridle rings or loops.

Some people prefer to use swivel clips to attach their flying lines to the bridles. This, however, adds to the overall weight, and an easier method is to connect the flying lines directly to the bridle loops using lark's-head knots.

A loop at the end of each flying line is secured to the bridle with a lark's-head knot.

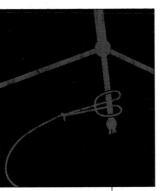

A knot tied at the end of the attachment point stops the lark's head from slipping off in flight.

Spar grabber (secures stand-off to spreader spar)

2 *To launch a swept-wing sport kite alone, first place a ground stake (a tent peg will do) firmly in the ground and loop one end of each flying line around it. Fully unwind both lines and make sure they are of equal length before connecting them to the kite's bridle. (If your lines are brand new, they may stretch fractionally during the first flight and need some further adjustment.) Prop the kite up so that it faces into the wind resting on its wingtips and stand-offs, then return to the ground stake and connect your flight straps to the other ends of the flying lines. You are now ready for takeoff.*

If you wish to leave your kite staked out in this manner for any length of time in a strong wind, it is always a good idea to lay it nose down so that it can't be launched by a sudden gust or wind shift.

Launching

3 Return to the handles and disconnect them from the ground stake, checking that there are no twists in the lines. Keeping your hands at waist level, take a step or two backward, pulling gently on the lines as you go, and the kite will rise into the air.

When the kite has climbed to its highest point, test the controls by pulling on each handle alternately, causing the kite to turn left or right, so that you become accustomed to the speed of turn.

Speed Control

Flying any stunt kite will be made easier by moving on the ground to control the forward air speed of the kite. By moving backward, you will accelerate the kite. Conversely, by moving toward the kite, you will slow it down, making dives and landings easier to execute.

4 A safe and easy method of landing the kite is to fly it as far as you can to your left- or right-hand side. At either extreme, the kite will be pointing into the wind where it will begin to stall, dropping gently to the ground.

As you fly horizontally from left to right, you will find that the pull of the kite varies, being apparently lighter at the edges than it is in the center. You will also find that as the kite climbs vertically it will reach a point, almost overhead, where its pull will ease off and it can be held stationary. This position will be useful for giving your arms a rest, especially if you are flying a power kite.

When you feel comfortable with the controls of the kite, you can try out some basic precision maneuvers (see pages 66–69).

Wind window

The area of wind in which a steerable kite will fly is called the Wind Window. Directly downwind of the pilot, the force of the wind on the kite's sail will feel stronger than it will when the kite is flown to the left or right of this "center window" position. This is because the kite is actually flying in an arc around the pilot (see Figure 1). As the kite approaches the left or right extremes of this arc, it will slow down as it begins to fly directly into the wind. The same variation in force will be apparent when the kite is flown vertically toward the top of the window (see Figure 2).

The main diagram on this page shows the wind window expressed as a shaded semicircle with a grid imposed on it. The darker the shading, the greater the force of the wind will feel and the faster the kite will travel (unless the pilot moves toward it to control its speed).

The grid simply indicates various points within the wind window and will help you to position your kite during the practice maneuvers that follow in this chapter.

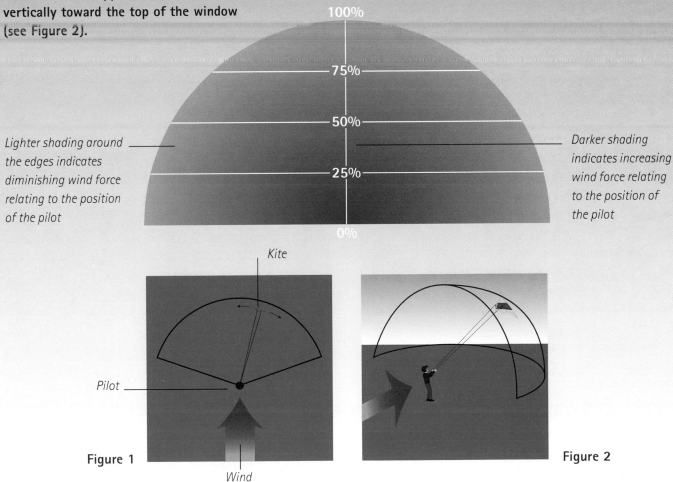

100%

75%

50%

Lighter shading around the edges indicates diminishing wind force relating to the position of the pilot

Darker shading indicates increasing wind force relating to the position of the pilot

25%

0%

Kite

Pilot

Figure 1

Wind

Figure 2

Small
upward loop
(see step 4 below)

1

4

2

3

Downward Loop

One of the easiest ways to get a feel for the controls of your kite is to effect this large, smooth turn, using steps 1 to 4 below as guidelines.

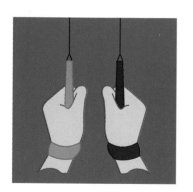

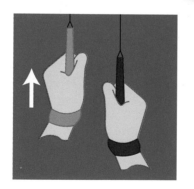

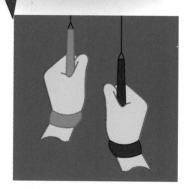

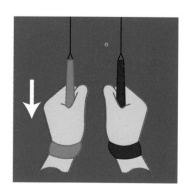

1 *Position the kite to begin this figure by flying it to a height approximately 75 percent up the wind window on the left-hand side. At this point, turn it to the right and, keeping your hands together, continue in a straight, horizontal line until you reach the window's center.*

2 *Push gently on the left-hand line to begin the loop, moving toward the kite as it begins to fly downward.*

3 *As the kite passes the ground at the lowest point of the loop, begin to move backward, helping it climb through the upward portion of the figure. Keep your hands steady, moving them only if the kite needs to be steadied on this circular course.*

4 *As the kite approaches the top of the loop, gently bring your hands together and exit the figure by continuing to fly in a straight, horizontal line to the left. You will now have a wrap in the lines which can be cleared by pulling on the left-hand line to fly a small upward loop.*

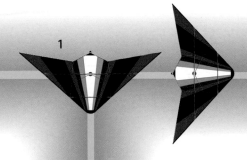

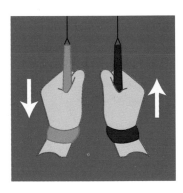

Square

In contrast to the previous figure, which required slow, fluid hand movements, the square needs to be flown with quick hand movements, but remember that only slight movements are needed to control the kite. The entry point for this figure is the same as for the circle, that is 75 percent up the wind window on the left-hand side.

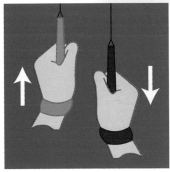

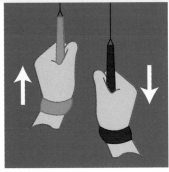

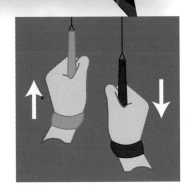

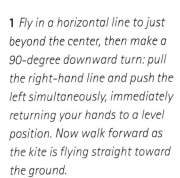

1 *Fly in a horizontal line to just beyond the center, then make a 90-degree downward turn: pull the right-hand line and push the left simultaneously, immediately returning your hands to a level position. Now walk forward as the kite is flying straight toward the ground.*

2 *When the kite is at a height of about 25 percent in the wind window, make another 90-degree turn using exactly the same push-pull hand movements. This time, however, there is no need to walk forward since the kite is traveling level with the ground.*

3 *The third turn will set the kite on the upward leg of the figure, and you will have to move backward to help the kite maintain speed as it climbs.*

4 *When the kite has reached the height at which you began the figure, execute a final 90-degree turn. Now, keeping your hands together, exit the figure with a smooth, horizontal line.*

Right-hand leading-edge landing and takeoff

To land the kite on its leading edge, simply fly it in a downward diagonal line toward the right-hand side of the wind window, walking forward as you do so. Remember that the stronger the wind, the faster you will have to move toward the kite to control its speed. When the leading edge of the kite comes to rest on the ground, push the left handle forward, tilting the kite back slightly to steady it and stop it from flipping over.

To take off from this position, gently pull the left-hand line until the kite is on the point of falling toward you. Then, taking a few steps backward, pull on both lines together and the kite should lift off again. This part of the maneuver requires quite subtle handling and may need to be practiced until it comes naturally. Handling will vary according to the model of stunter and the strength of the wind.

Like the other maneuvers in these pages, this can be flown in reverse.

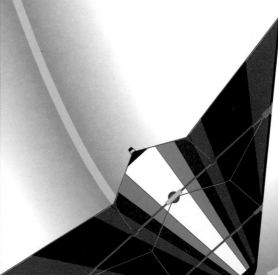

Wingtip landing

To land the kite on its wingtips, you will first need to stall it. When the kite is about 6 ft (2m) from the ground, push one hand forward with a punching motion, rapidly followed by the other, while swiftly moving forward. This motion will knock the air out of the kite's sail, and as you continue to move toward the kite, it should sink to rest on its wingtips.

More exaggerated hand movements combined with faster forward motion may be required to land the kite in a stronger wind.

Like other maneuvers described in this section, it will be easier to practice wingtip landing in light wind. Alternatively, if the wind is too strong to land the kite directly in the center of the window, this can be practiced on the left-hand or right-hand edge of the window.

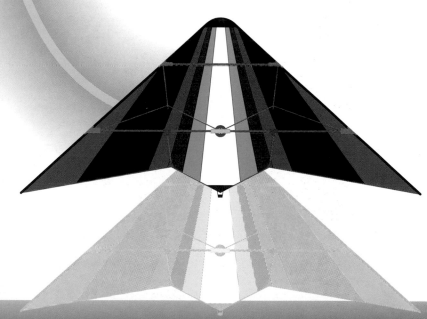

Launching and flying a Flexifoil power kite

FLYING TIPS

LOCATION
Wide open space free of ground-level obstructions

NUMBER OF PEOPLE NEEDED
One

SUITABILITY FOR CHILDREN
The small 4-foot Flexifoil is suitable for children aged 8 up

DEGREE OF DIFFICULTY
Among the easiest sport kites to learn on. However, larger Flexifoils or stacks do require some flying experience

ESSENTIAL ACCESSORIES
Smooth low-stretch sport line, padded wrist straps

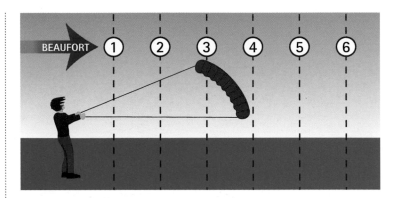

This 6-ft (1.8m) Flexifoil has only one spar which is made up of two tapered fiberglass rods. These are connected together with a brass ferrule and should be secured at the joint with tape. The spar is then inserted into a pocket which runs the length of the leading edge, and the 150-lb (70kg) flying lines are attached to each end.

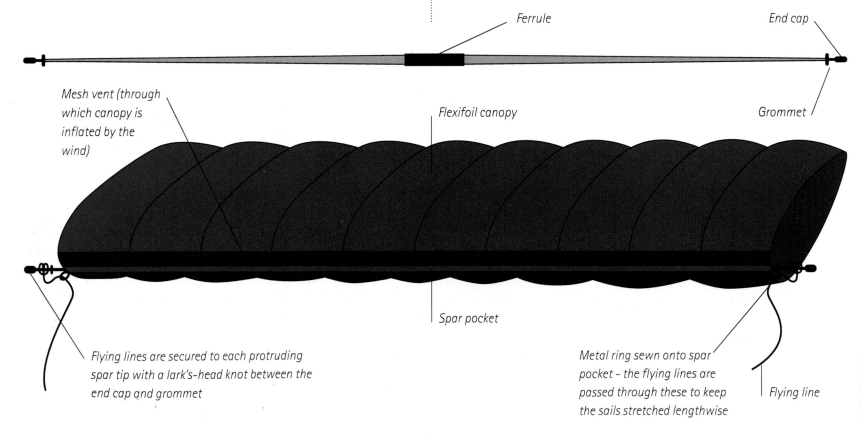

Ferrule

End cap

Mesh vent (through which canopy is inflated by the wind)

Flexifoil canopy

Grommet

Spar pocket

Flying lines are secured to each protruding spar tip with a lark's-head knot between the end cap and grommet

Metal ring sewn onto spar pocket - the flying lines are passed through these to keep the sails stretched lengthwise

Flying line

Launching

Flexifoils tend to pull more than most other types of kite, so you may find yourself leaning back to take the force. It may also be advisable to use padded wrist straps for extra comfort.

Having unwound and attached your flying lines, lay the kite upside down so that the aerofoil is inverted and it cannot take off. When you are ready to launch, pull on one line until the kite has swung around so its leading edge is pointing away from you. In this position the wind will flip the sail over so that the aerofoil is the right way up. Continue to pull the kite around until the vent is facing you. Then pull gently on both lines with equal pressure and the kite will inflate and take off.

A Flexifoil is steered using exactly the same left-and-right hand movements as a swept-wing stunter, but its graceful, sweeping turns tend to require more reach.

Because of the extra pulling power exerted by this type of aerofoil wing kite, you may find that it helps to rest your arms occasionally by steering the kite to any position on the edge of the wind window (see page 65). This will be particularly useful if you happen to be using larger or stacked kites in a strong wind.

The basic flying figures on the following pages will help you get a feel for the way in which this often-powerful kite performs.

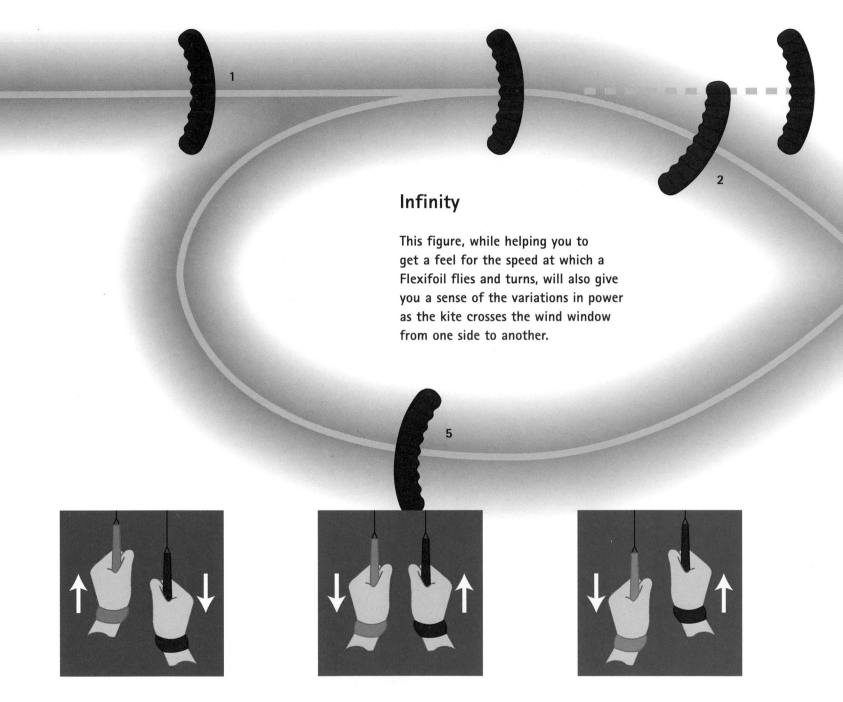

Infinity

This figure, while helping you to get a feel for the speed at which a Flexifoil flies and turns, will also give you a sense of the variations in power as the kite crosses the wind window from one side to another.

1 *Enter the figure at 75 percent high in the window, from the left, keeping both hands level, then pull on the right-hand line and gently push the left-hand line forward as you begin the figure. To achieve full use of the wind window, do not make this first downward turn too steep.*

2 *Smoothly return your hands to a level position to continue this downward diagonal leg of the figure. As the kite crosses the center of the wind window, you will feel its power increase and may need to lean back, supporting your body weight by placing one leg behind the other.*

3 *You are now approaching a point about 25 percent high on the right-hand side of the wind window, where you will begin to maneuver the kite through an upward turn by pulling the left-hand line back and pushing the right-hand line forward. Remember to make smooth transitional hand movements to maintain the continuity of the curves in this figure.*

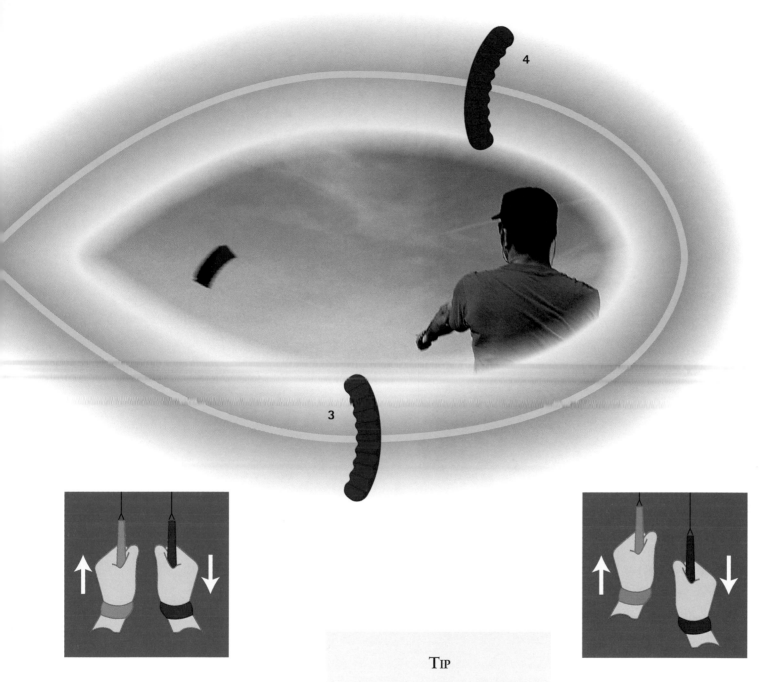

4 *When the kite has climbed in a curve to a point about 75 percent high on the right-hand side of the window, you will need to bring your hands level again so that you can align the kite to fly the second downward diagonal in much the same way as the first was flown, and crossing its path in the center of the window.*

TIP

If you are using a Flexifoil power kite for the first time, fly in a moderate wind, as the kite's power and speed can increase dramatically in strong wind.

5 *When the kite has reached a point 25 percent high at the left-hand side of the window, pull your right hand back and push your left hand forward so that the kite turns upward and flies through a curve until it has reached the point at which you first entered the figure.*

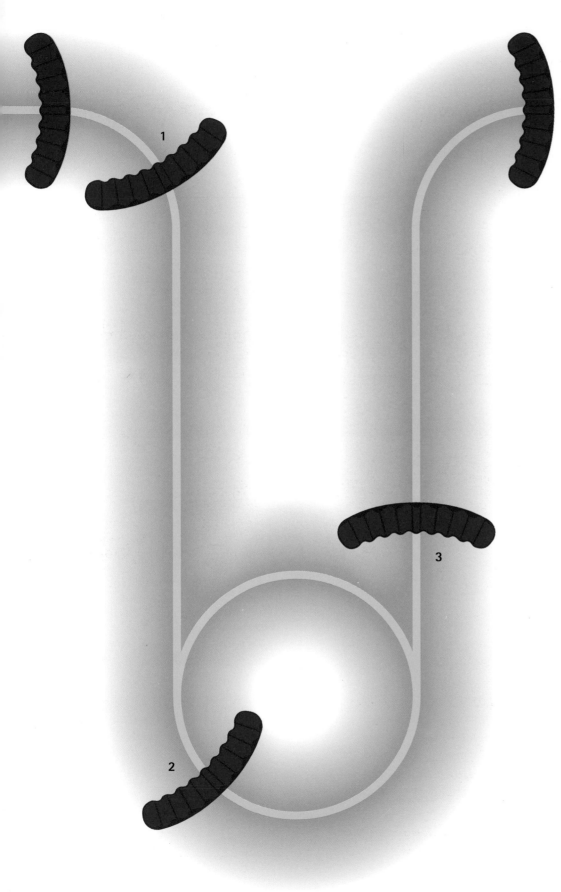

Power Dive and Roll

First check that there is no one in the path of the kite since you will be flying directly toward the ground at considerable speed.

1 *Enter the figure from the top left of the wind window, and turn the kite toward the ground by pushing your left hand forward and pulling you right hand back simultaneously. Bring both your hands together, allowing the kite to descend in a straight line. Speed control is optional here, depending on how brave you are feeling.*

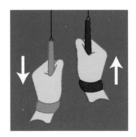

2 *When the kite is at a height of about 6ft (2m) above the ground, pull hard on the left side and push on the right simultaneously; hold this hand position until the kite has turned, describing the circle shown in the diagram. When flying this figure for the first time, execute the turn at a height about 25 percent high in the window for safety's sake.*

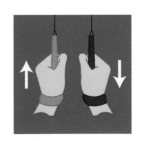

3 *Bring both hands together, and the kite will climb back vertically to the top of the wind window.*

Launching and flying a stack of Flexifoils

Flexifoils can easily be stacked together, in a ladder formation, to produce more power. The kites are linked by a series of stacking lines with a distance of approximately 6ft (2m) between each kite. The strength of flying line will have to be increased to allow for the extra pull.

Stacks of Flexifoils are commonly used for pulling buggies, boats, skates, or skis.

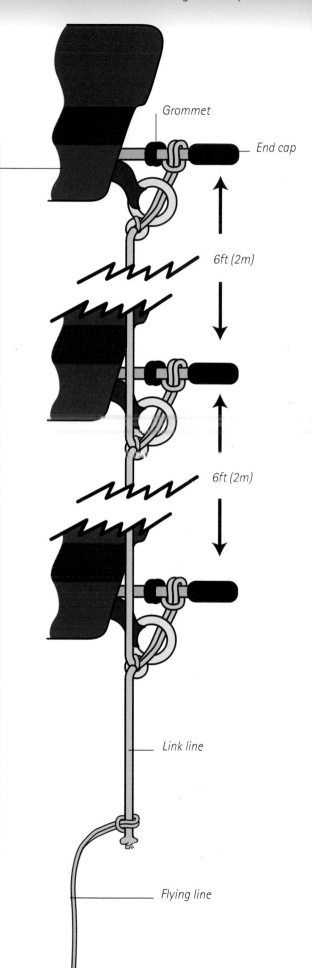

Grommet

End cap

6ft (2m)

6ft (2m)

Link line

Flying line

1 *It helps to have a co-pilot handy when launching a stack of Flexifoils as the usual flip-launch method could be complicated by the addition of extra kites. Once the kites and lines have been set up, it will be the job of the co-pilot to make sure each separate canopy has been inflated by the wind, since uneven inflation will cause the stack to wobble out of control. It is also important that the link lines are of exact equal lengths, since an unbalanced stack of kites will be extremely difficult to tame, particularly in a strong wind, and could even be dangerous.*

2 *Once the stack is airborne, it will move at the same speed as a single kite but with massively increased power. For this reason it is always a good idea to test-fly a stack in moderate wind. Once you are in control of the stack, you can try flying the Infinity figure in a strong wind. This motion will keep the kite powered up enough to drag you downwind. The experience is known as "scudding," and can be safely controlled by bending the knees and leaning back against the force of the kite. Bear in mind that it may wear down the soles of your shoes.*

Launching and flying a quad-line Revolution

FLYING TIPS

LOCATION
Often flown on short lines, so ideal for urban parks or any other suitable flying sites

NUMBER OF PEOPLE
One

CHILDREN
5-ft (1.5m) Revolution could be flown by a 10-year-old

DIFFICULTY
Requires concentration and practice as hand movements differ from conventional two-line kites

ESSENTIAL ACCESSORIES
Smooth low-stretch sport line, ground stake

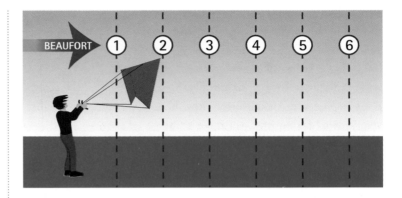

The Revolution will challenge your flying skills since its four-line control system makes it one of the most sensitive steerable kites. The following tips will give you a basic introduction to quad-line technique.

1 *Assemble the Revolution by joining together the carbon-fiber leading-edge spars and locating the two vertical spars. Unwind the lines and clip them onto the kite's bridle in the top and bottom positions. Attach the other ends of the flying lines to the corresponding loops at the top and bottom of each curved alloy handle.*

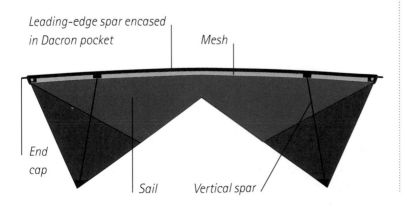

Leading-edge spar encased in Dacron pocket

Mesh

End cap

Sail

Vertical spar

2 *To launch a Revolution, set the kite upright on the ground, as shown. Hold the handles so that the fingers are resting near the top, with the fingertips of each hand spread down the padded section of the handles. This will give you a greater degree of control. Keeping your hands close together, tilt the handles backward, take a step backward, and the kite should rise off the ground.*

Tilt handles back

Tilt handles forward

3 *To reverse the kite, simply tilt the handles forward again and it will fly backward to its landing position. Although this sounds unbelievably simple, you will find that the slightest deviation in hand movement will make the kite do something that you hadn't anticipated. The secrets of successful Revolution flying are patience, relaxation, concentration, and a lot of practice. The reward is hours of the most mind-absorbing style of flying yet available.*

4 *Once you have mastered the vertical launch and land technique, you might want to start building up a repertoire of other maneuvers. Try tilting one handle backward and the other forward. This will cause the kite to pivot on its central axis. To stop the motion, align the handles again and tilt them the other way to reverse the spin.*
    Try flying this maneuver in slow motion, stopping the kite at intervals as it turns. This may prove more difficult, but it will increase your degree of control.

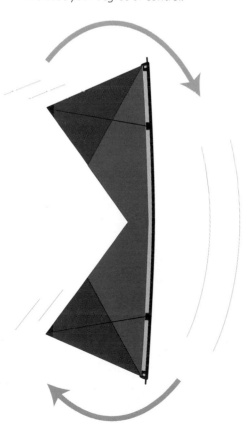

Tilt your left handle back and your right handle forward to make the kite spin in a clockwise direction.

To spin the kite counter-clockwise, tilt your left handle forward and your right handle back.

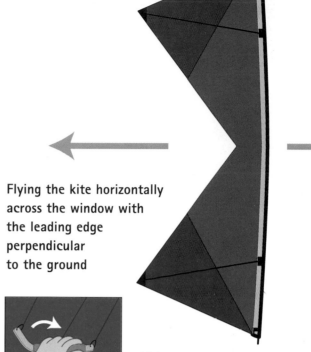

Flying the kite horizontally across the window with the leading edge perpendicular to the ground

If the leading edge is on the right of the trailing edge, your left hand will be slightly above your right hand. Tilt both handles backward to move forward.

Tilt both hands forward to reverse the kite, keeping the leading edge in a vertical position perpendicular to the ground.

6 *One of the fundamental skills in Revolution flying is to hold the kite stationary for any length of time in any part of the wind window. This is a matter of sensing the balance of the kite. From a stationary position, you can explore the effects of an almost infinite range of hand movements until you are in total control of the kite.*

The length of flying line used with a Revolution will have a considerable effect on the speed of the kite. The shorter the line used, the faster the kite will seem to respond to the controls. (Many quad-line pilots choose to fly on lines over about 50ft [15m] in length.)
    The same axiom applies to dual-line kites, through it is worth bearing in mind that longer lines (say, 100 ft [30m]) make it easier for the flyer to learn the basic methods of control.

Make your own kites

Building your own kite
need not be a difficult task.
In fact, many kite fliers claim that
the greatest satisfaction comes
from flying their own creations.
The sled kite has been chosen as
an introductory project because
of its total simplicity, and is
followed by eight other designs
of increasing complexity.

Tools and Materials

Many of the materials illustrated on these pages can be bought from specialist kite stores. (A worldwide list of kite retailers appears on pages 122 and 123.) Ripstop nylon is used in the manufacture of spinnaker sails and can also be obtained from most boating suppliers.

If you need to substitute any of these recommended materials, look for alternatives that are lightweight but durable. Sail material should have as little stretch as possible in a strong breeze. Spars should be able to flex slightly without breaking, as they may be under stress during flight.

The tools required for kite making can usually be found in hardware stores or at notions counters. A sewing machine is not essential since seams can be stitched together by hand using a needle and thread, but this could turn out to be a rather laborious task, especially in the case of the soft stunter, which has numerous seams.

As a rule, nylon kites should always be stitched together, as it is unlikely that any form of glue will withstand the force of air pressure.

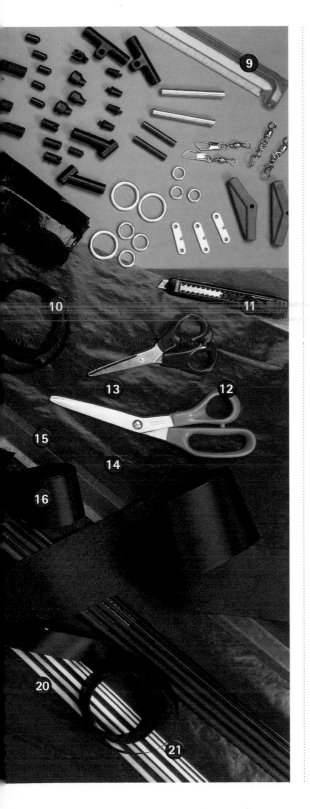

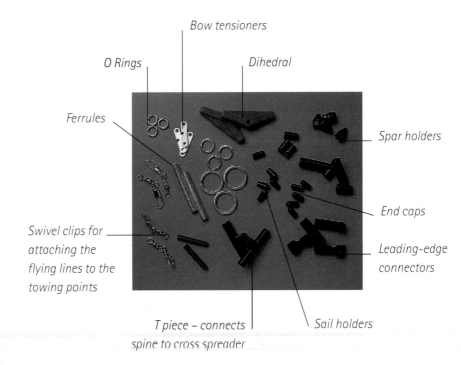

Bow tensioners

O Rings

Ferrules

Dihedral

Spar holders

Swivel clips for
attaching the
flying lines to the
towing points

End caps

Leading-edge
connectors

T piece – connects
spine to cross spreader

Sail holders

1 Tracing paper

2 Masking tape

3 Polyester sewing
thread is compatible
with ripstop nylon

4 Ripstop nylon is
available in a wide
choice of colors and
combines the desired
weight and strength
for kite building. A
fine grid is woven
into the fabric to
retard stretching
and tearing

5 Soldering iron

6 Hole punch

7 Cardboard for making
templates

8 Plastic trash bags can
be used as a kite-
making material, but
choose only those
which are made of
high-density plastic to
avoid stretch

9 Ruler

10 Bungee cord

11 Craft knife

12 Fabric scissors

13 Small scissors for
use in cutaway
appliqué designs

14 Tissue paper

15 Dacron reinforcing tape

16 Yardstick

17 Carbon-fiber spars

18 Glue (white craft glue
will do)

19 Hacksaw

20 Wooden spars

21 Fiberglass spars

The degree of difficulty varies quite a lot among the nine kites in this chapter, but the following star rating will help you to identify at a glance what processes are involved in making each kite:

Quick and easy. No sewing required

The sail is easy to make, but the frame is a little more tricky. No sewing required

Sewing required

Sewing required. Bridle adjustment is critical, especially in the case of the small stunter

Very precise cutting and sewing required. Multiple twin bridle may need fine adjustment

Trash-bag Sled

This Sled is a perfect workshop or classroom project kite as it can be made in less than half an hour from very basic materials.

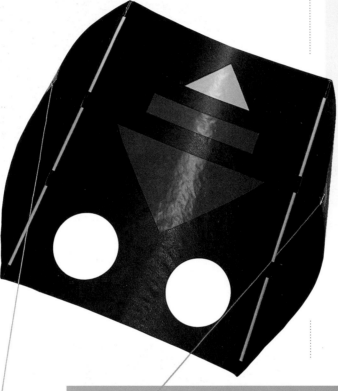

YOU WILL NEED

1 clean high-density plastic trash bag

2 x 18in (2 x 45cm) x 3/16-in (4mm) diameter wooden dowel or garden stake

Strong tape

50ft (15m) nylon or cotton string, breaking strain approx. 20-35-lb (10-15kg) test

1 sheet thin cardboard

Colored shopping bags (optional)

Measuring tape

Pencil

Craft knife

Hole punch

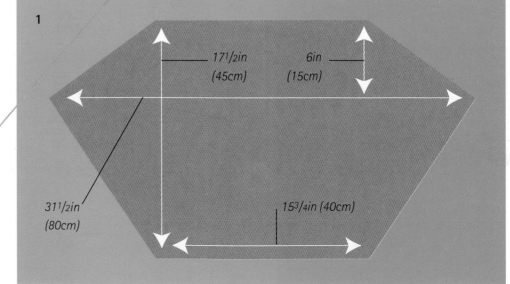

1

17¹/₂in (45cm)   6in (15cm)

31¹/₂in (80cm)

15³/₄in (40cm)

1 *Mark on a sheet of thick cardboard the shape and dimensions shown in the diagrams. This will become the template for the kite's shape.*

Cut it out and place it on a fully outstretched trash bag. Cut all the way around. This will give you the basic Sled shape.

(By using a template, you can cut through several layers of plastic at once to produce a number of kites.)

2 *Using 1-in (2.5cm) lengths of tape, secure the spars in the positions shown in the diagram.*

3 *Reinforce the outer wingtips using 1-in (2.5cm) strips of tape and punch a small hole at the corner of each wingtip. The reinforcing tape on the wingtips is vital, since the bridle line will be tied at these positions.*

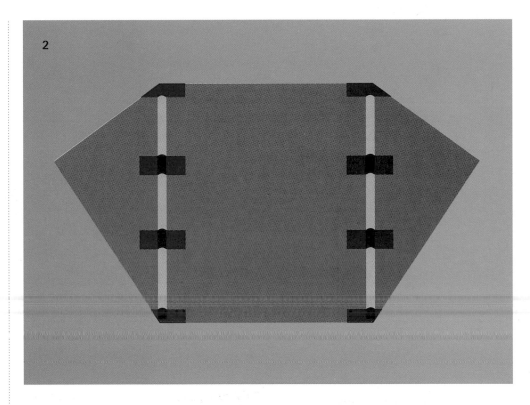

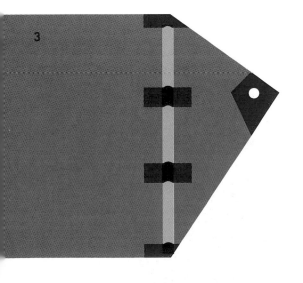

4 *Measure and cut a piece of string three times the width of the kite from corner to corner (in this case, it will be 8ft [2.4m] long). Tie one end securely to each of the two reinforced wingtips.*

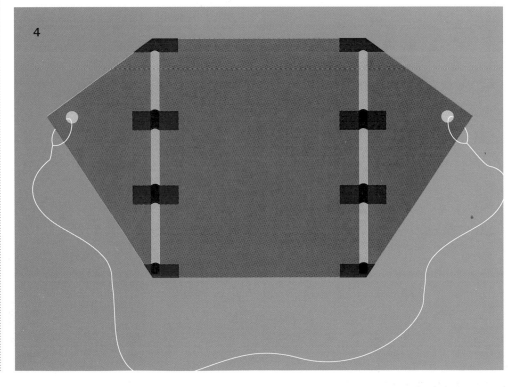

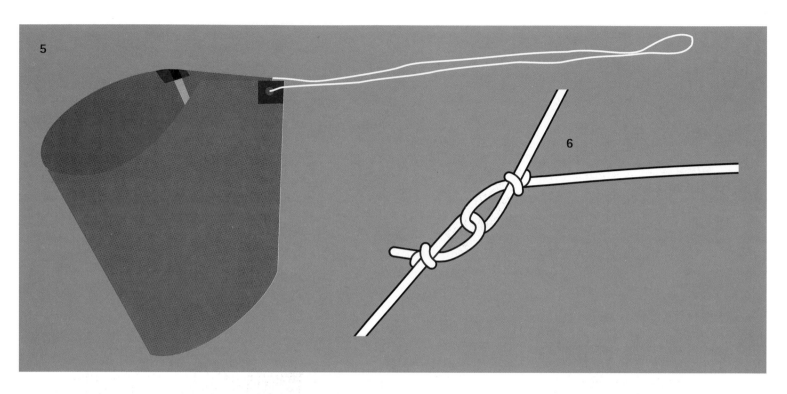

5 *Find the center of this bridle line by folding the kite in two from wingtip to wingtip and pulling the line taut. Tie a 1-in (2.5cm) loop* *at this point, to which the flying line can then be attached. Alternatively, an O ring can be lark's headed to the bridle.*

6 *Secure the end of the flying line to the loop in the bridle, and the Sled is ready to fly. You may wish to use a swivel clip.*

If you don't already possess a kite reel, a suitable alternative can be made from an empty liquid detergent bottle. There is no need to adapt the bottle in any way to suit this purpose (see diagram), but if you fill it with sand to weigh it down, it can also act as a good ground anchor.

DID YOU KNOW?

Kites can be scaled up or down provided that material weight and strength are taken into consideration.

In fact, the biggest Sled ever made was built by a team of enthusiasts in Holland in 1980. It stood a gigantic 45ft (14m) high and had a span of 75ft (23m).

TIPS

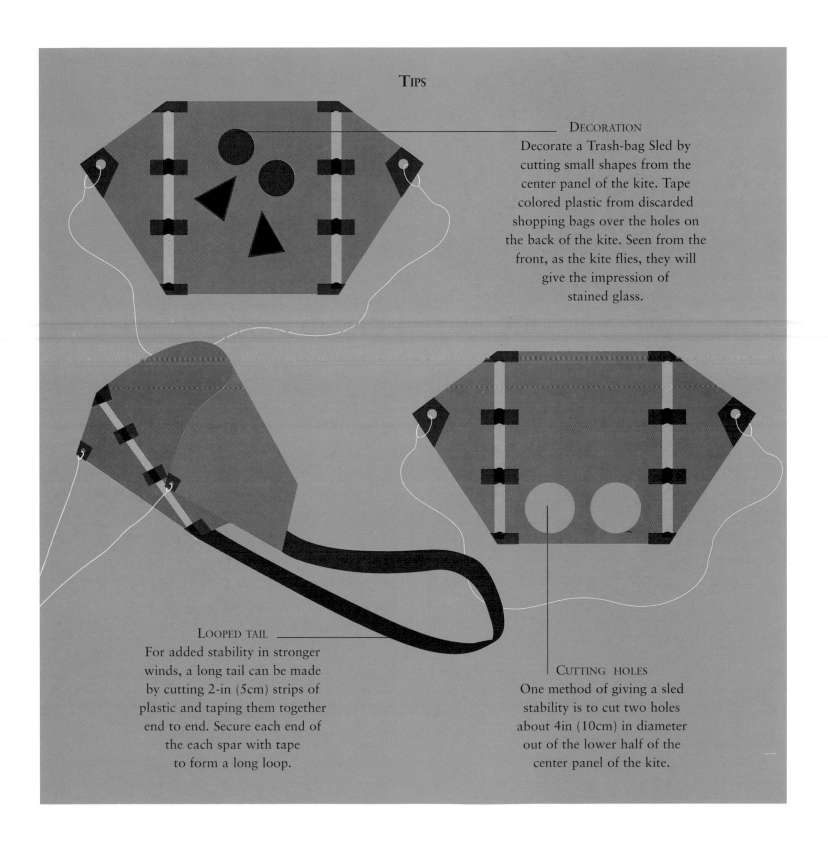

DECORATION

Decorate a Trash-bag Sled by cutting small shapes from the center panel of the kite. Tape colored plastic from discarded shopping bags over the holes on the back of the kite. Seen from the front, as the kite flies, they will give the impression of stained glass.

LOOPED TAIL

For added stability in stronger winds, a long tail can be made by cutting 2-in (5cm) strips of plastic and taping them together end to end. Secure each end of the each spar with tape to form a long loop.

CUTTING HOLES

One method of giving a sled stability is to cut two holes about 4in (10cm) in diameter out of the lower half of the center panel of the kite.

Square dancer

This little kite is a simple variation of an Indian fighter and can be put together in a matter of minutes to yield hours of fun. Though it can easily be scaled up, a larger version may need stronger construction methods like those used in the Malay on pages 96–99.

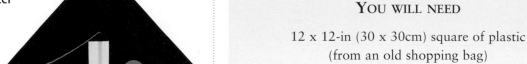

YOU WILL NEED

12 x 12-in (30 x 30cm) square of plastic
(from an old shopping bag)

17in (43cm) x $^3/_{16}$-in (4mm)-diameter wooden dowel

20in (51cm) x $^1/_8$-in (3mm)-diameter
flexible fiberglass rod

50ft (15m) nylon/cotton string,
breaking strain approx. 20-35-lb (10-15kg) test

Strong tape

Scissors or craft knife

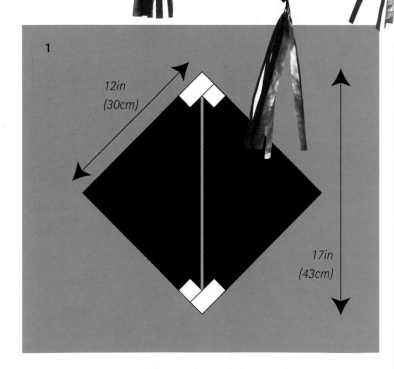

12in (30cm)

17in (43cm)

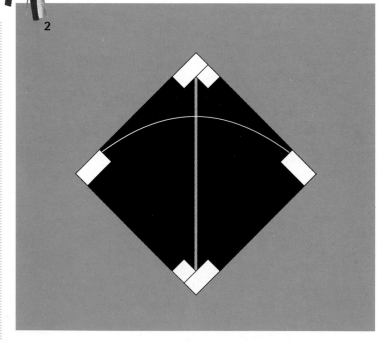

1 Cut out the plastic to make a square. Lay it flat and place the wooden dowel, or spine, so that it lies diagonally across it, as illustrated. Secure the spine in this position by taping it to the top and bottom corners of the sail, folding the tape over onto the front of the sail so that the spine is attached securely.

2 Tape one end of the fiberglass rod to each of the two outer wingtips, to form a cross spreader. Again, fold the tape over onto the front of the sail. You may need to use a double layer of tape at these points as they will have to be strong enough to bear the extra pressure of the flex in the cross spreader.

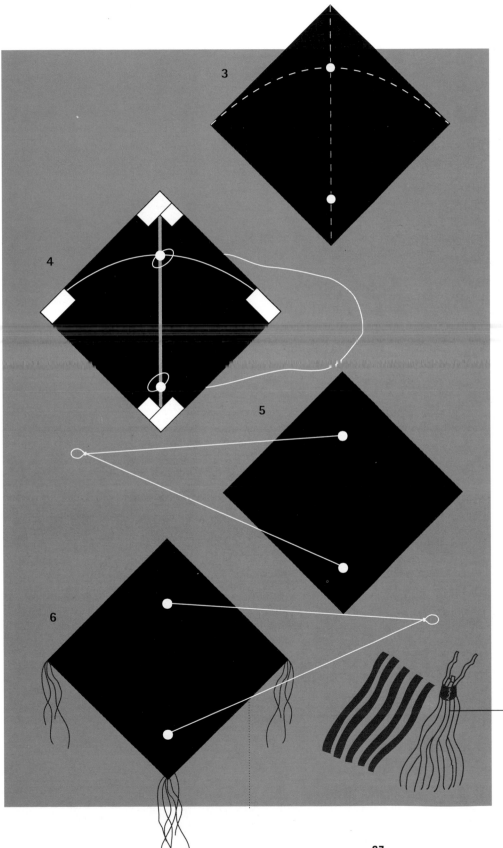

3 Turn the kite over and make two small holes, one at the junction of the spine and cross spreader, and another 1in (2.5cm) from the base of the spine. To add reinforcement at these points, stick a patch of tape at the estimated positions, then punch the holes through the tape.

4 Make a bridle for the Square Dancer: cut 1yd (1m) of string and tie it to the spine at the positions shown, first threading each end of it through the top and bottom holes in the sail. Remember to loop the top of the bridle line around both the spine and cross spreader.

5 Set the flying angle of the kite by stretching the bridle out as shown until the top leg is lying just below the horizontal, then tie a loop as an attachment point for the flying line. The position of this loop can be altered to accommodate different wind speeds (as is the case with the Pipa on pages 88–90).

6 To add a finishing preflight touch, you might want to make some tassel tails from any surplus plastic. These, though not absolutely critical to the aerodynamics of the design, will lend it a bit of panache.

Cut a number of strips from leftover plastic and bind them together at one end with tape. Bind a length of string to the tassel as shown so that the two protruding ends can be used to tie the tassel to the kite in the positions shown in step 6.

Brazilian Pipa

Pipas are usually made from tissue paper and bamboo, but they can be constructed just as easily from tracing paper and 1/4-in (6mm) wooden dowel. For this kite, nylon string is ideal since it stretches slightly, which will help keep the frame of the kite under tension during its construction.

I was taught how to make this traditional kite by a Brazilian student whose expert demonstration took only 20 minutes.

YOU WILL NEED

Tracing paper

1/4-in (6mm)-diameter bamboo or dowel (see below for length)

50yd (50m) nylon/cotton string, breaking strain approx. 10-lb (5kg) test

Craft glue

Small hacksaw

Craft knife

Scissors

Measuring tape

Pencil

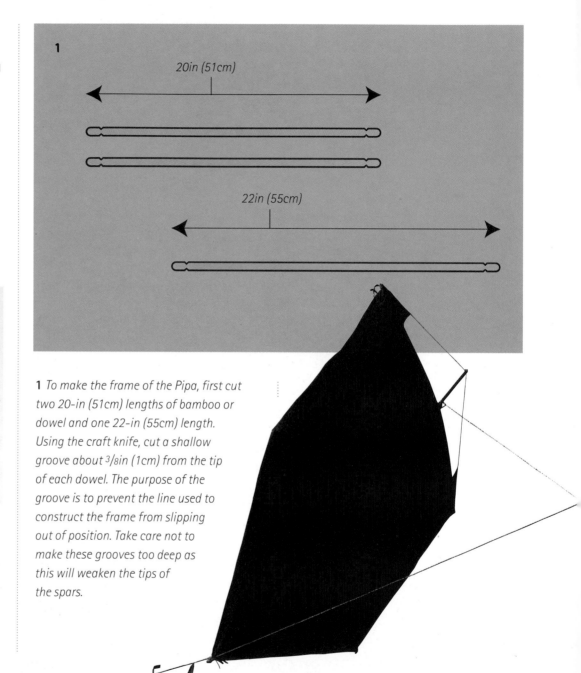

1 *To make the frame of the Pipa, first cut two 20-in (51cm) lengths of bamboo or dowel and one 22-in (55cm) length. Using the craft knife, cut a shallow groove about 3/8in (1cm) from the tip of each dowel. The purpose of the groove is to prevent the line used to construct the frame from slipping out of position. Take care not to make these grooves too deep as this will weaken the tips of the spars.*

An alternative method is to make a slit at the tip of each dowel, and then, having passed the line through it, bind some string around it to prevent the spar from splitting (see the instructions under How to Make a Wind Hummer on page 91).

2 Using the string, tightly bind one of the shorter spars (cross spreaders) 2³/₄in (7cm) from the tip of the longest spar to form a cross. Then continue to wind the string down the longest spar (the spine) in a diagonal spiral until you reach a distance of 8¹/₂in (22cm) from its other end. At this point, bind the second spar to the spine and again continue to wind the string down the spine until you reach the notch at the bottom. Bind the string tightly around this notch, three or four times, to maintain tension on each cross-spreader junction before moving on to the next step.

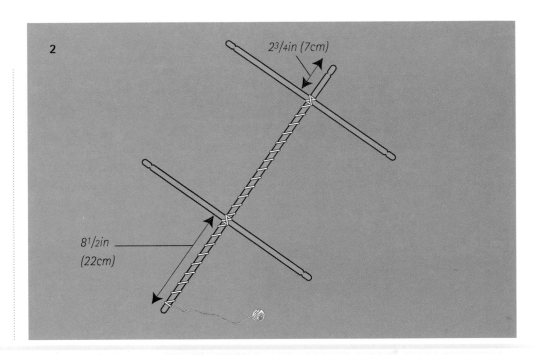

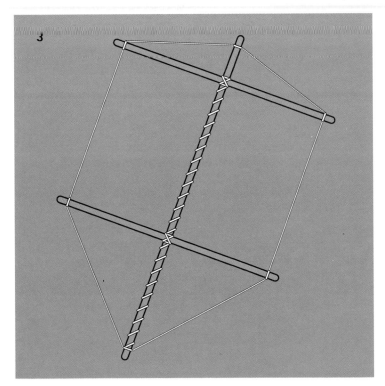

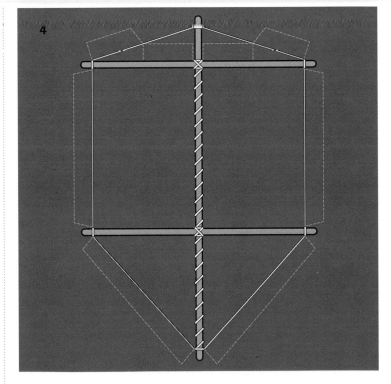

3 Wind the string once around the frame, wrapping it around each notch as you go until a string perimeter is formed. The string should be taut, but too much tension will cause the frame to distort. Tie the perimeter string at the base of the spine and trim off any surplus.

4 Lay the frame on a sheet of tracing paper and cut around the shape of the frame as shown, leaving a border of about 1¹/₂in (4cm) all the way around. Trim a V-shaped notch from the border at each spar tip as shown.

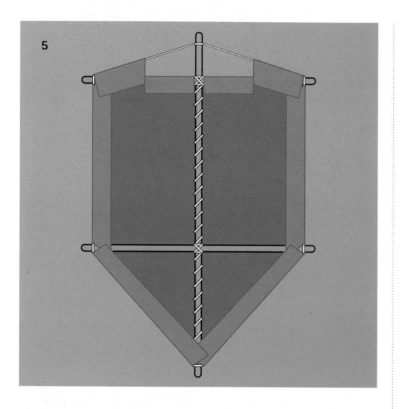

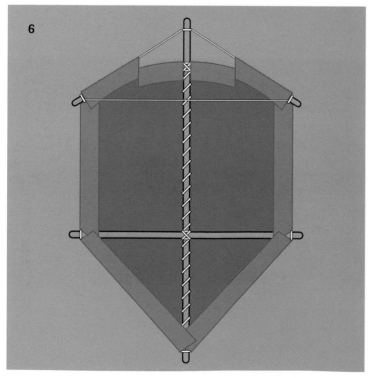

5 *Fold the edges of the paper over the string that is stretched around the perimeter and glue it in position. You may also apply glue to the string perimeter so that the folded edges of the paper stick to it as well.*

6 *While you are waiting for the glue to dry, why not make a tail for the kite? Cut any surplus paper into strips (see Tail Tips opposite). Then cut a piece of string to a length of about 13ft (4m) and tie these paper strips to it at intervals of approximately 2in (5cm). (You may need a couple of extra sheets of paper.) The resulting tail can be secured to the base of the kite's spine with a knot.*

A paper-tassel tail like this will have the effect of stabilizing the kite, particularly in stronger winds. A Pipa can, however, be flown without a tail, although it will have a tendency to rock from side to side.

7 *When the glue has dried, the kite is ready to be bowed into shape. This is done by tying a length of string to one end of the top spreader, stretching it across the back of the kite, flexing the top spreader as you do this, then tying the other end to the opposite spar tip. This bow string should keep the curved spar under tension. Be careful not to put too much tension on the top spreader, or it will be likely to spin in flight. On the other hand, too little tension will render the kite unstable whether or not it is flown with a tail.*

At this stage it is possible to attach a simple hummer device to the kite's frame: see opposite.

8 *Finally, you will need to make a bridle for the kite. Cut a 40-in (105cm) length of string. Tie one end of it to the junction of the spine and top spreader, and the other end to the base of the spine. To set the bridle at an appropriate flying angle, stretch it out to one side of the kite so it forms a V shape with one edge lying parallel to the top spreader. When it is in this position, tie a loop as shown on page 87 so that you have a towing point to attach the flying line.*

Remember that the position of this loop may have to be adjusted to compensate for the wind's strength. If the kite seems unstable in a strong wind, then try moving the loop about 3/8in (1cm) toward the nose at the top of the kite. Alternatively, in a light wind, the loop may have to be moved down about 3/8in (1cm) toward the tail.

How to make a wind hummer

Kites are sometimes fitted with hummers, which make a
buzzing sound as they fly. The Malaysian Wau Bulan on page 36
is a classic example of a kite bearing its own musical device.
A simple form of hummer can be made by stretching a
length of flat tape from one end to the other of a wooden or
bamboo rod, so that the tension in the tape causes the rod to flex
or bow. The tighter the tape is, the higher the pitch of sound
produced will be. It is important, however, that the overall
weight of the hummer can be lifted easily by the kite to
which it is fitted.

*Fitting a simple form of hummer to a
Pipa is just a matter of stretching a
length of tape (discarded audio-cassette
tape will do) across the upper horizontal
spar in place of the string tied there in
step 7 to bow the spar.*

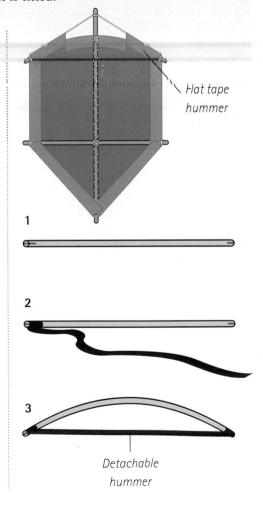

Flat tape
hummer

Making a
detachable hummer

1 *Take a 1-yd (1m) length of ¼-in (6mm)
bamboo and cut a notch at each end.*

2 *Secure the end of a length of cassette
tape to one end of the bamboo, first
passing it through the notch to prevent it
from slipping under tension.*

3 *Pass the tape through the notch at the
other end of the bamboo and pull it tight
so that the spar flexes. When you have
the desired tension, tie the tape securely
around the end of the spar and trim off
any excess. The hummer is now ready to
be tied to the spine of the kite.*

1

2

3

Detachable
hummer

Tail tips

To make the tail of a Pipa, roll
a sheet of paper lengthwise, press
it flat, and cut into strips about
1in (2.5cm) wide. Unfold the strips
and follow step 6.

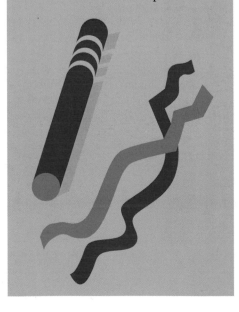

Mini Barroletta

This is a tiny version of the giant Barrolettas that grace the skies of Guatemala on All Saints' Day. Little kites like this one are made and flown by children all over Central America.

YOU WILL NEED

A piece of cardboard

3 or 4 sheets of colored tissue paper

5 x 13-in (34cm) lengths of garden stake (not more than 3/16in (4mm) in diameter)

A spool of sewing thread

Paper glue

Scissors and a craft knife

A reel of 10-lb (5kg) test flying line

1 *Mark the center of each stake and cut a small notch at both ends of each one using a craft knife.*

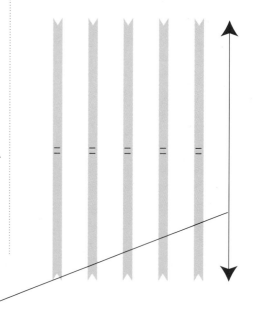

13in (34cm)

92

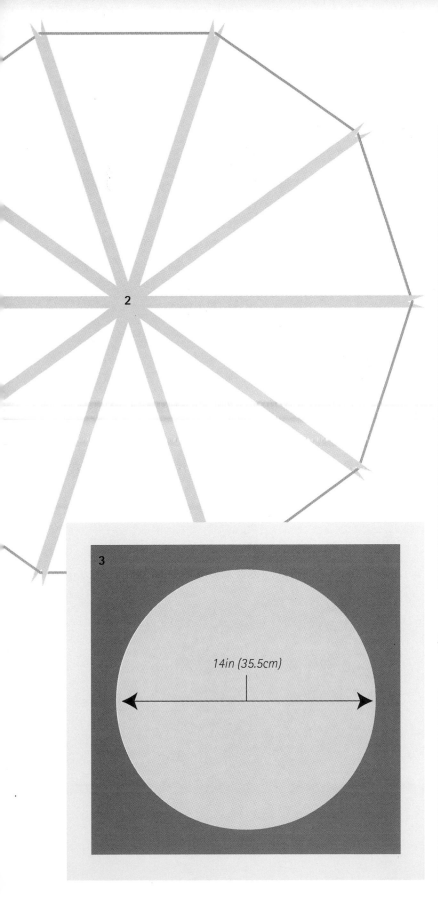

2 *Tie the five spars together at the center, so that they cross to form a shape like the spokes of a wheel. Bind them as tightly as you can to minimize any movement. Now run a length of sewing thread around the tips of the spars, passing it through the notch in each as you go.*

3 *Cut a circle 14in (35.5cm) in diameter from cardboard to use as a template for the sail. Lay it on top of one of the sheets of tissue paper and cut all the way around it.*

4 *Lay the frame of the kite flat on the circle of tissue paper and fold the rim of the paper over the string perimeter, gluing it down as you go. A small fold at the tip of each spar will hold the sail flat against the frame.*

14in (35.5cm)

5 *The front of the kite can easily be decorated by cutting shapes from surplus tissue paper and gluing them onto the sail. Not only will these shapes enhance the kite, they will also serve to reinforce it in strategic places, such as the spar tips and the points at which the bridle is tied to the frame.*

ALTERNATIVE PATTERNS

No two Barrolettas have the same pattern. Designs are simply appliquéed over the basic sail.

6 *To make tails for a Barroletta, first cut two 8-in (20cm) squares of tissue paper and slice them both at 1-in (2.5cm) intervals to a distance of 2in (5cm) from the end of each. These tassels can be extended by gluing more colored strips to the end of each. The complete tails are then glued to the rim of the kite as shown.*

ALTERNATIVE TAIL

If you decide to scale up this kite, it may need a longer and heavier tail like the one below.

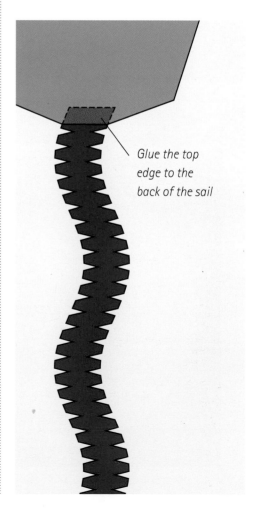

Glue the top edge to the back of the sail

GIANT BARROLETTAS

When these kites are made on a very large scale, as they are for the All Saints' Day festival in Guatemala, their frames are constructed using lengths of bamboo with a diameter of up to 2in (5cm). Extra reinforcement is given to a full-sized barroletta frame by a square of bamboo secured at its center. The sail is also made stronger by being made of several layers of plain tissue paper.

7 *Make a bridle for the mini Barroletta by cutting from the flying line one length of 40in (1m) and another of 20in (50cm). Fold the longer of the two in half and tie two knots about ¼in (5mm) apart. Now tie a loop at one end of the shorter line and lark's head it to the longer line between the two knots.*

8 *Pierce three holes in the positions shown in Figure 8. Pass each end of the longer line through the two holes in the kite's perimeter, and secure them to the spars. Now pass the shorter line through the central hole and secure it to the point at which the spars cross. Tie your flying line to the loop where the three bridle lines meet.*

7

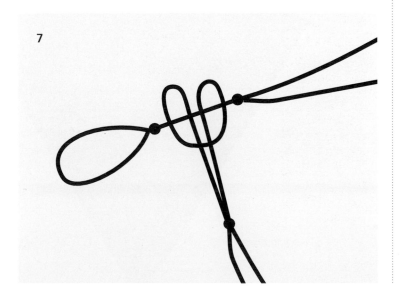

8

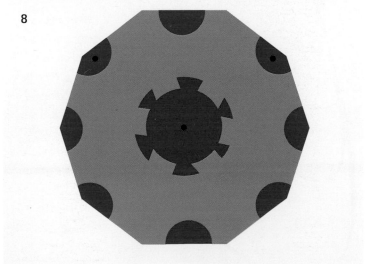

Malay

This is a classic diamond-shaped kite. In this incarnation the kite does not need a tail, but you can add one for decoration if you like. A few simple tail ideas can be found on page 99.

You will need

1 yard (1m) ripstop nylon

2 x 35in (90cm) x 1/4-in (6mm) diameter dowel

24in (60cm) Dacron tape, 1-in (2.5cm) wide

12in (30cm) seam tape, 5/8-in (1.5cm) wide

1 x 1/4-in (6mm) plastic dihedral

6ft (2m) x 88-lb (40kg) braided flying line

1 x 3/8-in (1cm) alloy ring

Pencil

Measuring tape

Scissors

2

Fold the tape in three

Then fold almost in half leaving a slight overlap

Stitch the sides of each pocket down

1 *Mark the sail on the nylon, and cut it out. There is 3/8in (1cm) allowed, all the way around, for a hem. Turn the hem under and machine stitch it in place.*

2 *Make the four spar pockets. Each of them is made from 6in (15cm) of 1-in (2.5cm) Dacron tape. Fold each piece of tape in three, and then almost in half. Then sew the pocket together down two sides as illustrated.*

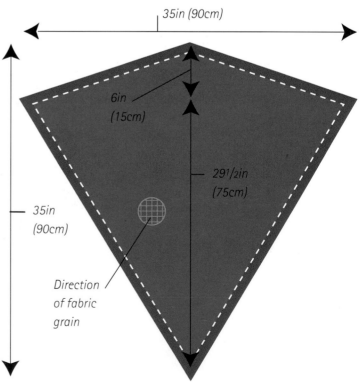

35in (90cm)

6in (15cm)

35in (90cm)

29 1/2in (75cm)

Direction of fabric grain

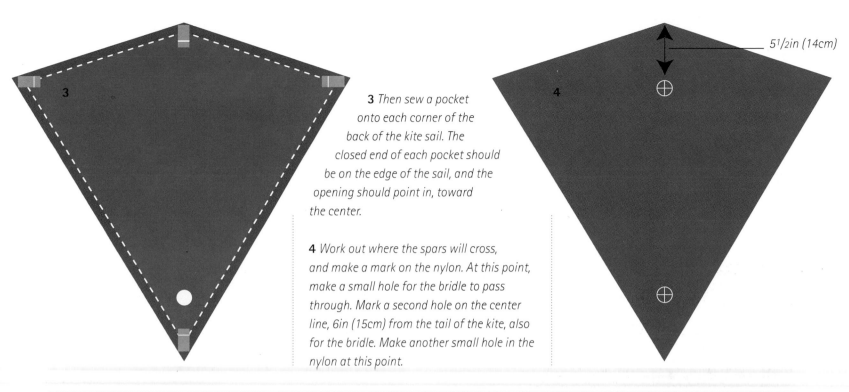

5¹/₂in (14cm)

3 *Then sew a pocket onto each corner of the back of the kite sail. The closed end of each pocket should be on the edge of the sail, and the opening should point in, toward the center.*

4 *Work out where the spars will cross, and make a mark on the nylon. At this point, make a small hole for the bridle to pass through. Mark a second hole on the center line, 6in (15cm) from the tail of the kite, also for the bridle. Make another small hole in the nylon at this point.*

HOW TO LIVEN UP YOUR SAIL

When you have cut out the basic sail shape of your Malay, you can decorate it with a pattern of colored shapes. This is done by cutting out the required shapes and sewing them onto the back of the sail. Then using a pair of small, sharp scissors, cut away the sail from inside each shape, taking care not to cut through the shapes themselves. Because ripstop nylon often has a slippery coating, it may help to moisten the surface of each shape before you stitch it into position. This will prevent the fabric from sliding out of alignment as it passes under the sewing machine needle.

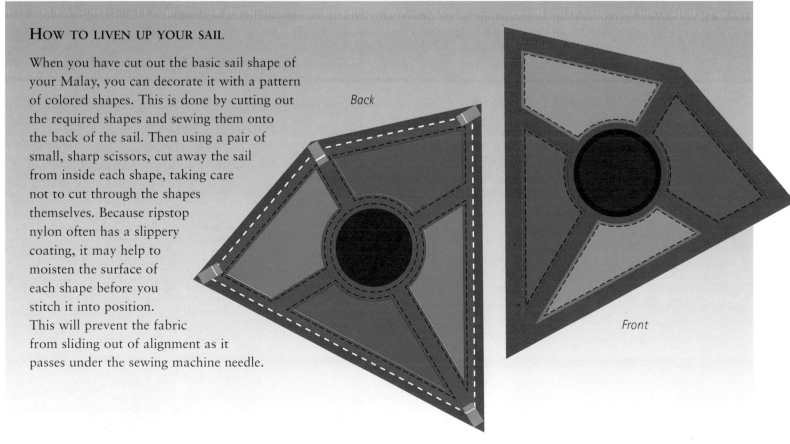

Back

Front

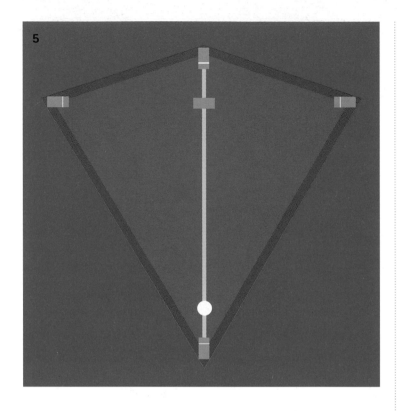

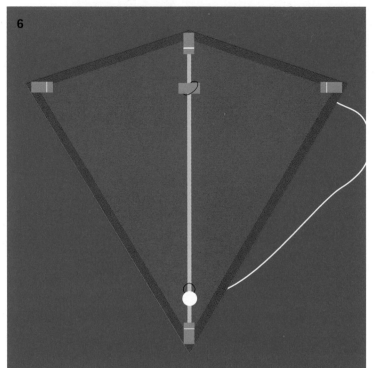

5 *Slip the dihedral piece onto the 35-in (90cm) dowel and fit this piece into the top and bottom pockets, trimming it back slightly, little by little, if necessary.*

6 *Align the dihedral over the top hole. Thread one end of the bridle line through and around the dihedral, and then back through the hole. Tie it firmly. Thread the other end of the bridle through the lower hole, around the spar, back through, and tie off.*

7 *Take the other piece of dowel and insert it into the dihedral. Pull the sail out, as tight as possible, and trim the wood to size so that it will fit tightly from the dihedral to the wingtip pocket. Take the dowel out and cut a second one exactly the same size.*

8 *Put both pieces of dowel back into the dihedral and wing pockets. They will be very tight, but this is correct, as ripstop nylon has a slight degree of stretch and will soon absorb the tightness. It is worth remembering this method of fitting spars; you may need to use it again to repair your kite.*

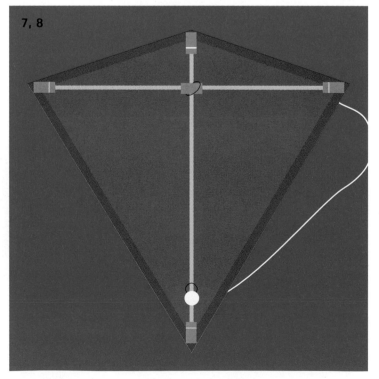

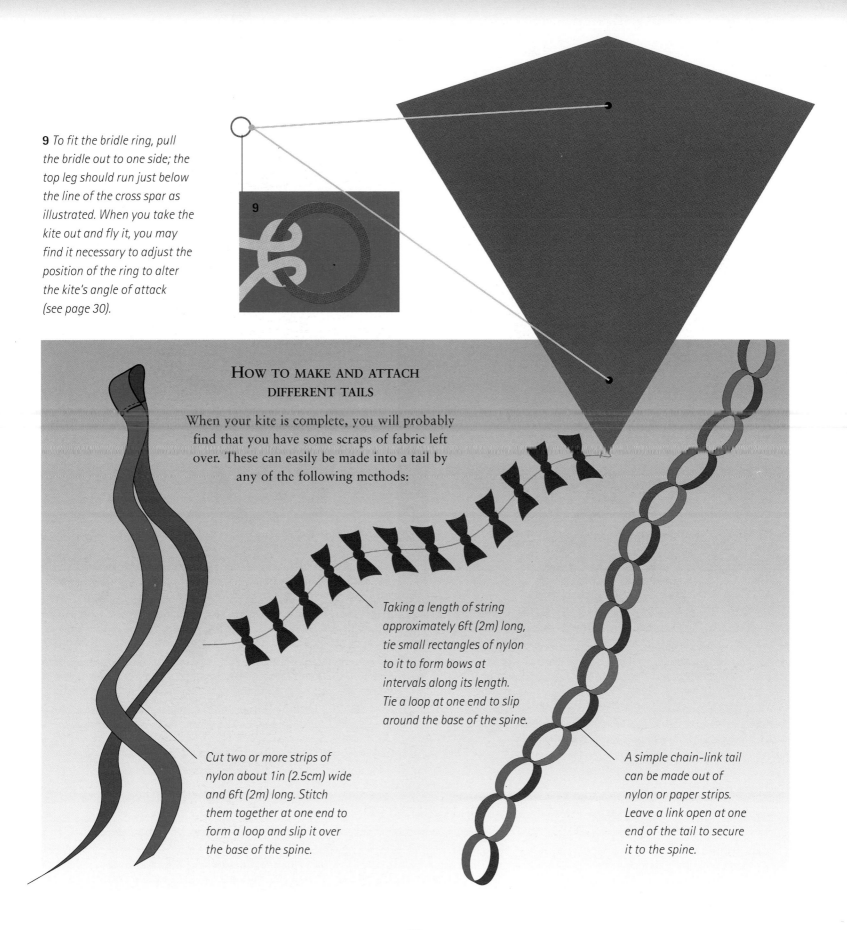

9 *To fit the bridle ring, pull the bridle out to one side; the top leg should run just below the line of the cross spar as illustrated. When you take the kite out and fly it, you may find it necessary to adjust the position of the ring to alter the kite's angle of attack (see page 30).*

HOW TO MAKE AND ATTACH DIFFERENT TAILS

When your kite is complete, you will probably find that you have some scraps of fabric left over. These can easily be made into a tail by any of the following methods:

Taking a length of string approximately 6ft (2m) long, tie small rectangles of nylon to it to form bows at intervals along its length. Tie a loop at one end to slip around the base of the spine.

Cut two or more strips of nylon about 1in (2.5cm) wide and 6ft (2m) long. Stitch them together at one end to form a loop and slip it over the base of the spine.

A simple chain-link tail can be made out of nylon or paper strips. Leave a link open at one end of the tail to secure it to the spine.

Box kite

Box kites are normally thought of as consisting of squares, but this kite is a little different and looks more like the famous Gibson Girl rescue kite from World War II.

Although it is preferable to use carbon–fiber rods for the cell spreaders, ordinary 1/4-in (6mm) dowel may be substituted with little effect on performance.

YOU WILL NEED

2 yards (2m) ripstop nylon

4 x 36in (90cm) x 1/4-in (6mm)-diameter dowels

Approx. 81/2ft (2.5m) x 1/8-in (3mm)-diameter carbon rod or 1/4-in (6mm)-diameter dowel
(This will be divided into four lengths: see below for details)

13 ft (4m) x 5/8in (1.5cm) seam tape

8 x spar holders: either 1/8in (3mm) or 1/4in (6mm), depending on cross spars used

2yd (2m) x 80-lb (36kg) braided flying line

1 x 3/8-in (1cm) alloy ring

Pencil

Measuring tape

Scissors

1 Mark and cut out the two cells of the kite, according to the measurements shown in the diagram. There is a 3/8-in (1cm) seam allowance along the top and bottom long edges for a hem. Fold this over and machine stitch in place.

59in (1.5m)

10⁵/8in (27cm)

Direction of fabric grain

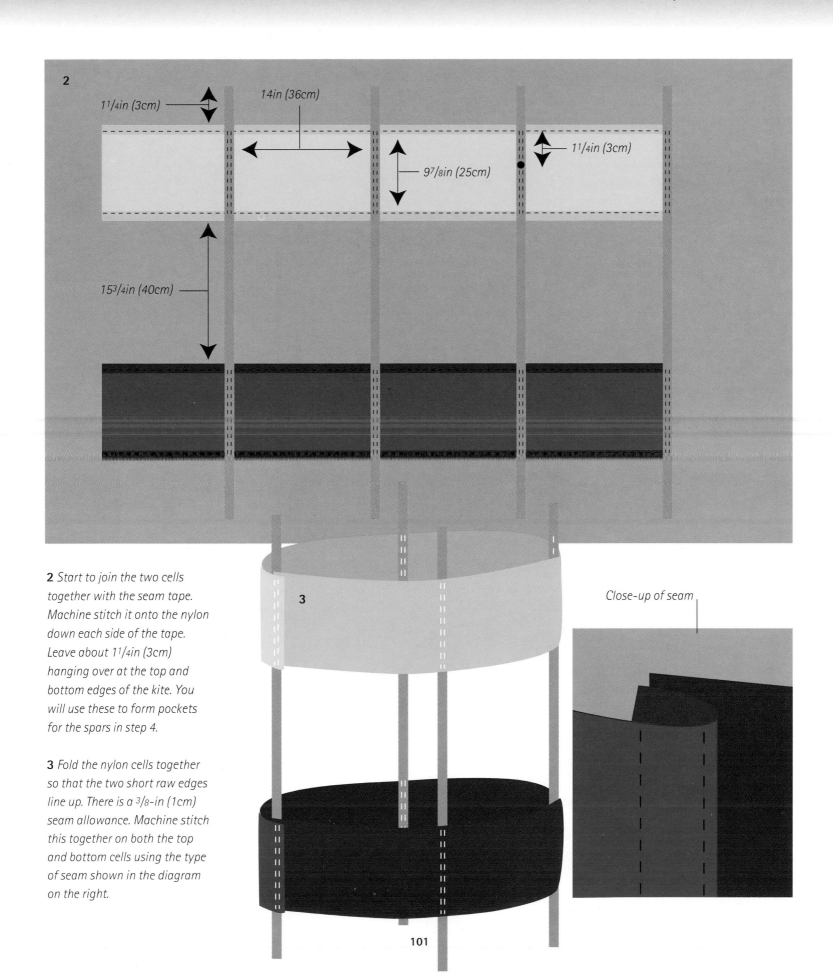

2 *1¼in (3cm)*

14in (36cm)

9⁷/₈in (25cm)

1¼in (3cm)

15³/₄in (40cm)

2 *Start to join the two cells together with the seam tape. Machine stitch it onto the nylon down each side of the tape. Leave about 1¹/₄in (3cm) hanging over at the top and bottom edges of the kite. You will use these to form pockets for the spars in step 4.*

3 *Fold the nylon cells together so that the two short raw edges line up. There is a ³/₈-in (1cm) seam allowance. Machine stitch this together on both the top and bottom cells using the type of seam shown in the diagram on the right.*

3

Close-up of seam

4 *Form the spar pockets by folding back the seam tape and neatly sewing down each side of it to make a pocket about 5/8in (1.5cm) long. On one seam cut a hole through the tape and the nylon 1¼in (3cm) down from the top of the kite: this is to thread the bridle line through when tying it to the frame.*

5 *Attach a spar holder to each end of the four cross spreaders. Insert the four wooden dowels into the pockets at the top and bottom of kite. Then insert the cross spars. These should be slightly curved when you assemble the kite so that the fabric is stretched taut. In order to get this slight curve, you have to start off with the cross spars about 10 percent longer than simple arithmetic would suggest. Start at 18in (45cm) and trim down both spars a tiny amount at a time until the fit is correct.*

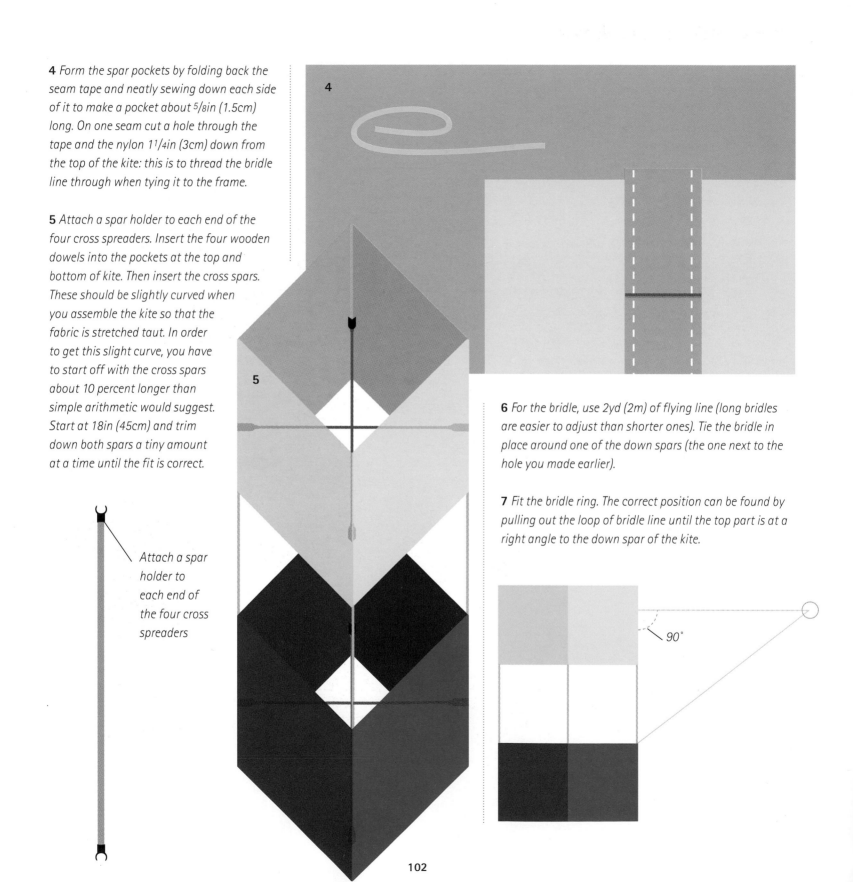

Attach a spar holder to each end of the four cross spreaders

6 *For the bridle, use 2yd (2m) of flying line (long bridles are easier to adjust than shorter ones). Tie the bridle in place around one of the down spars (the one next to the hole you made earlier).*

7 *Fit the bridle ring. The correct position can be found by pulling out the loop of bridle line until the top part is at a right angle to the down spar of the kite.*

90°

How to make a basic drogue

A drogue is like a small windsock in appearance and is attached to a kite in the same manner as a tail to give it stability in strong or turbulent wind. The front opening of a drogue is wider than the opening at its rear end, so that when wind flows into it a certain amount of pressure builds up, generating a drag force. As a general rule, larger kites require longer drogues to increase drag and therefore stability.

The following drogue is easy to construct and can be scaled up for use with larger kites.

YOU WILL NEED

20in (50cm) ripstop nylon

4ft (1.2m) x 30-45-lb (15-20kg) test line

Swivel

Binding tape

Scissors

1 Cut four panels to the dimensions shown (these dimensions allow for seams).

2 Sew the four panels together along their longest sides and stitch a length of binding tape around the widest end. Hem the narrow end.

3 Cut four 1 x 2-in (2.5 x 5cm) rectangles of ripstop nylon and fold each one in three (see Figure 3) to form tabs.

4 Using a couple of rows of stitches for added strengh, sew the tabs to the binding tape at the bottom opening of the drogue, using the seams as a guide to position them. A scaled-up drogue will need more tabs.

5 Take the line and divide it in half, then turn the drogue inside out and tie the ends of the two halves of line to opposing tabs. Finally, make a loop where the lines meet and attach a swivel using a lark's-head knot.

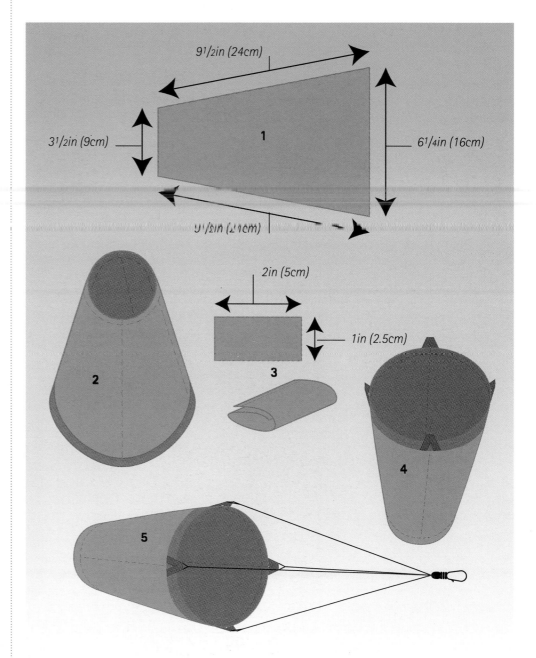

91/2in (24cm)

31/2in (9cm)

61/4in (16cm)

2in (5cm)

1in (2.5cm)

Rokkaku

This is a design by Carl Robertshaw, former European sport-kite champion and well-known British kite designer.

All measurements can be scaled up or down if you want to make a larger or smaller Rokkaku.

The Rokkaku, a traditional Japanese fighting kite, has become popular among kite flyers all over the world. Though traditionally made of washi (a very fibrous traditional Japanese paper) and bamboo, a stronger version can be made from modern materials to suit a variety of climatic conditions and withstand the rigors of battle.

YOU WILL NEED

35 x 50in (90 x 125cm) piece(s) heavy paper or cardboard

40 x 60in (100 x 150cm) ripstop nylon

1yd (1m) Dacron tape, 1in (2.5cm) wide

400ft (120m) x 65-lb (30kg) flying line (also used in the kite construction)

Soldering iron

2 bow tensioners

1/4-in (6mm) arrow knock

2 x 35-in (90cm) x 1/4-in (6mm)-diameter dowel ("short")

1 x 50-in (125cm) x 1/4-in (6mm)-diameter dowel ("long")

O ring

Pencil

Sharp scissors

Small hacksaw

1 *Copy the template to size onto heavy paper or cardboard, then cut along the solid black lines so that you have four triangles and one rectangle. This gives you a template from which to cut the ripstop nylon.*

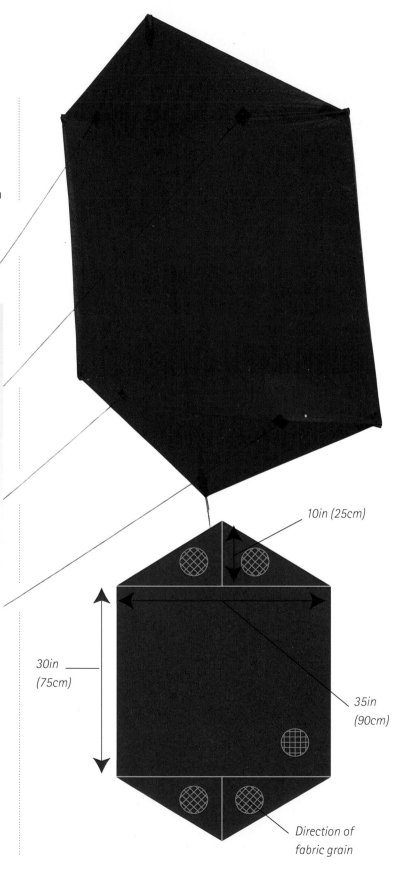

10in (25cm)

30in (75cm)

35in (90cm)

Direction of fabric grain

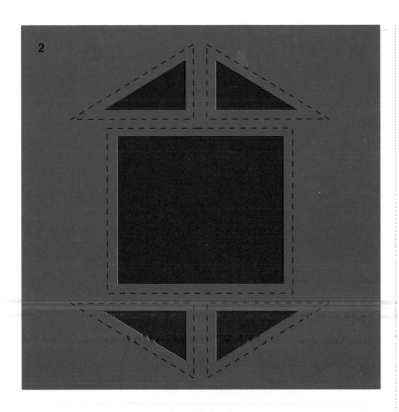

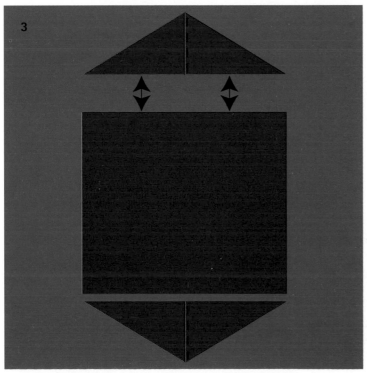

2 *Place the templates on the ripstop nylon, with the grain running in the direction indicated on the plan. Using the pencil, draw around the five templates, leaving ⅝-in (1.5cm) seam allowance right around the edge of each piece. Cut out the five panels from ripstop nylon using a pair of sharp fabric scissors.*

Rolled seam

3 *Sew the panels together with a ⁵/₈-in (1.5cm) rolled seam. To make a rolled seam, put the pieces together with the raw edges aligning. Stitch ⁵/₈ in (1.5cm) in from the raw edges, then roll the seam over, tucking under the edges and stitch again along the resulting fold. Start with the top two triangles, then the bottom two; then join the top to middle section, and finally the middle to the bottom. This makes the hexagonal Rokkaku sail. Sew a rolled hem around the whole sail to make a neat border. Doing this will also give the finished kite some extra strength, should it be flown in battle.*

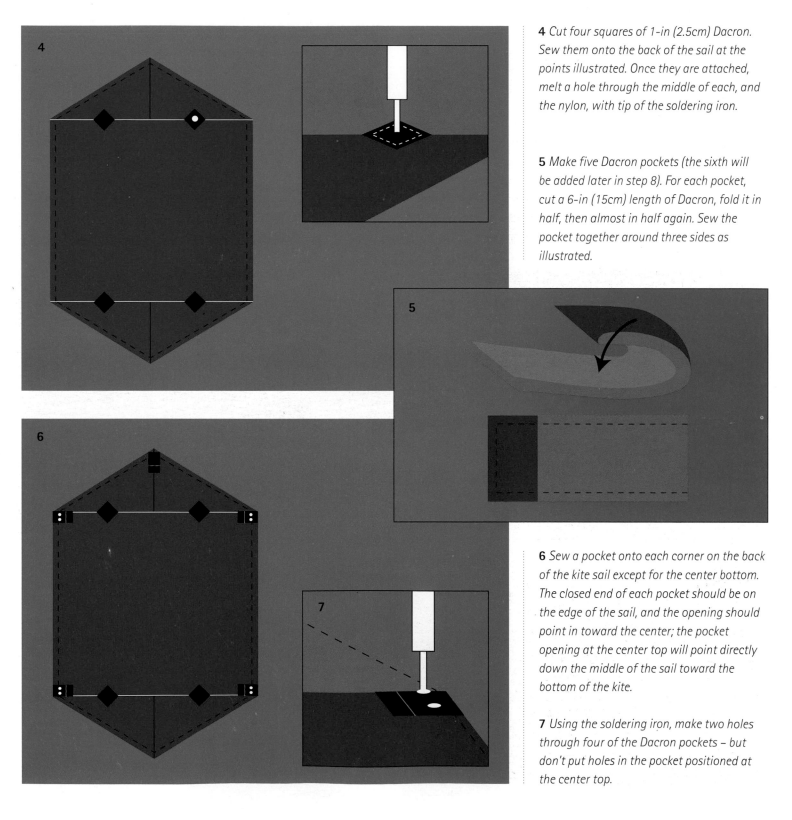

4 *Cut four squares of 1-in (2.5cm) Dacron. Sew them onto the back of the sail at the points illustrated. Once they are attached, melt a hole through the middle of each, and the nylon, with tip of the soldering iron.*

5 *Make five Dacron pockets (the sixth will be added later in step 8). For each pocket, cut a 6-in (15cm) length of Dacron, fold it in half, then almost in half again. Sew the pocket together around three sides as illustrated.*

6 *Sew a pocket onto each corner on the back of the kite sail except for the center bottom. The closed end of each pocket should be on the edge of the sail, and the opening should point in toward the center; the pocket opening at the center top will point directly down the middle of the sail toward the bottom of the kite.*

7 *Using the soldering iron, make two holes through four of the Dacron pockets – but don't put holes in the pocket positioned at the center top.*

8 *Cut another Dacron strip, this time 2in (5cm) long, and sew it onto the bottom center corner of the sail at the back (on the same side as all the other pockets), and make two holes in it with the soldering iron as illustrated in step 7.*

9 *Cut two lengths of the flying line 51in (130cm) long. Taking one of the lengths, thread one end through both holes in a top side pocket and tie it securely, so that the excess line hangs on the back of the kite. Thread the other end of the line through a bow tensioner, then slide it through both holes on the opposite top pocket and back to the bow tensioner. Repeat this step with the second length of line you cut, except this time attach them to the two bottom opposite pockets.*

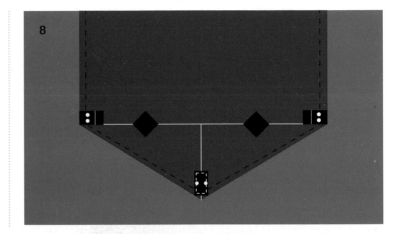

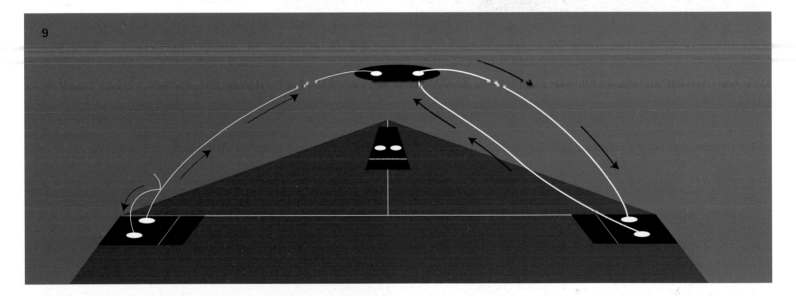

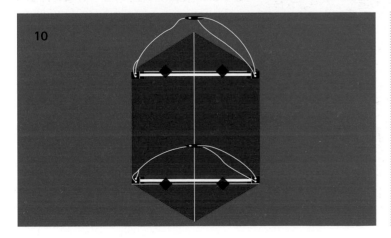

10 *Insert the ends of a 35-in (90cm) "short" dowel into the top two pockets on the back side of the sail, and then do the same with the other short dowel in the bottom two pockets.*

As the purpose of the spars in any kite is to maintain tautness in the sail, it is usually a good idea to cut the spars a little larger than necessary. This means you can make fine adjustment to the length by trimming them, little by little, to fit the sail – as described under the Box Kite (see step 5, page 102).

Once in place, these two shorter dowels need not be removed again unless they happen to break, as the kite can be rolled around them for storage.

11 *Insert one end of the 50-in (125cm) "long" dowel into the top center pocket, inside the bow lines, leaving them "free" to make the bow in the two "short" dowels. Put the 1/4-in (6mm) arrow knock on the bottom end of the "long" dowel.*

12 *Cut a 4-in (10cm) length of line. Thread it through the bottom center holes and tie it to make a loop. Hook the loop on the other arrow knock, and tighten the loop to achieve the maximum possible tension in the sail. Once the kite has been flown several times, it may be necessary to readjust this tension as the sail will probably stretch slightly.*

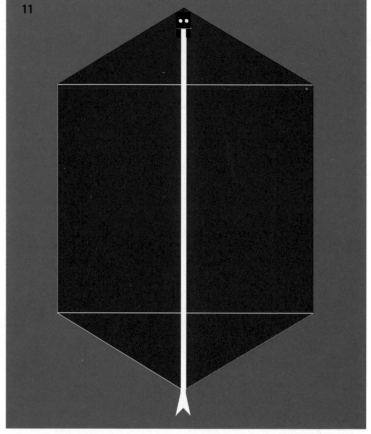

Front view

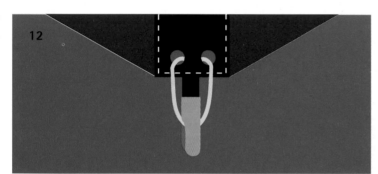

Back view

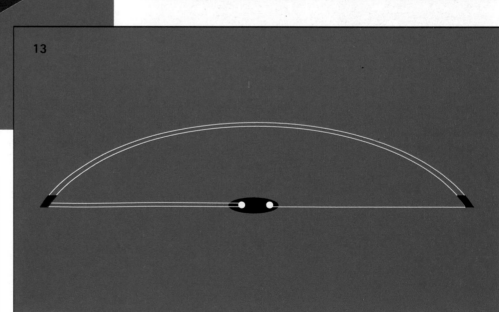

13 *Slide the bow tensioner along the bow line, causing the cross spreaders to curve so that a distance of 3 1/2in (9cm) can be measured between the spine and the bow string illustrated. This position of the bow tensioner can be marked on the string in ink, as a guide. Slight variations in the depth of bow may be needed to finetune the kite.*

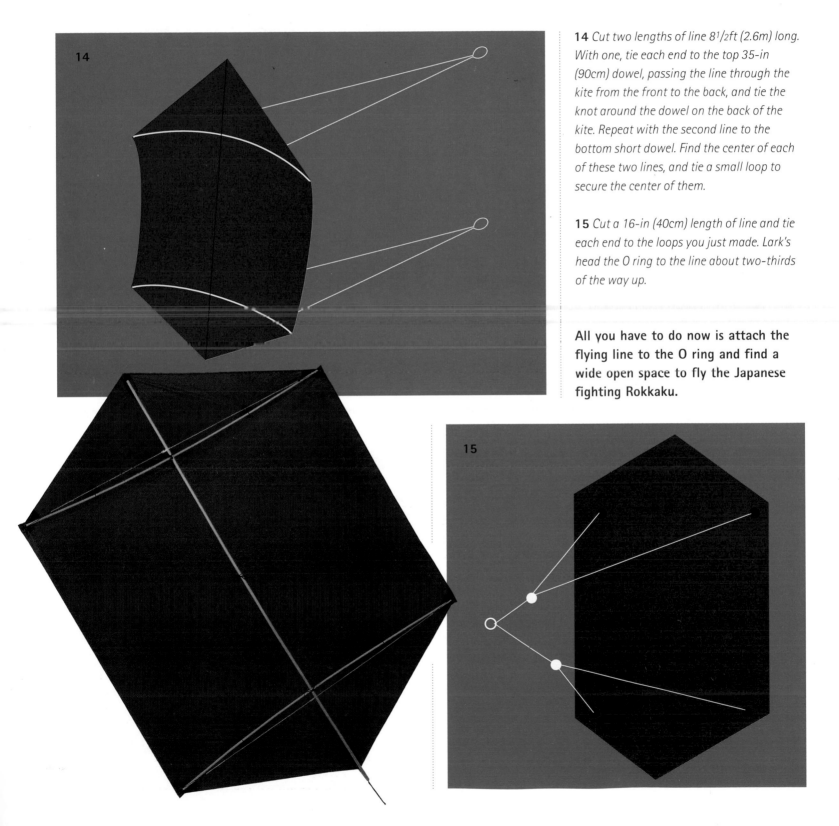

14 *Cut two lengths of line 8¹/2ft (2.6m) long. With one, tie each end to the top 35-in (90cm) dowel, passing the line through the kite from the front to the back, and tie the knot around the dowel on the back of the kite. Repeat with the second line to the bottom short dowel. Find the center of each of these two lines, and tie a small loop to secure the center of them.*

15 *Cut a 16-in (40cm) length of line and tie each end to the loops you just made. Lark's head the O ring to the line about two-thirds of the way up.*

All you have to do now is attach the flying line to the O ring and find a wide open space to fly the Japanese fighting Rokkaku.

★★★★

Small swept-wing stunt kite

This small stunt kite is designed to use solid 3/16-in (4mm)-diameter carbon-fiber spars and reflects construction methods used in full-size stunt kites with a span of 8ft (2.4m).

There are three stages of construction: making the sail, assembling the kite, and test flying to determine the correct bridle setting. A stunter of this size will require approximately 8 miles (13km) an hour of wind to fly and will respond quickly to the controls.

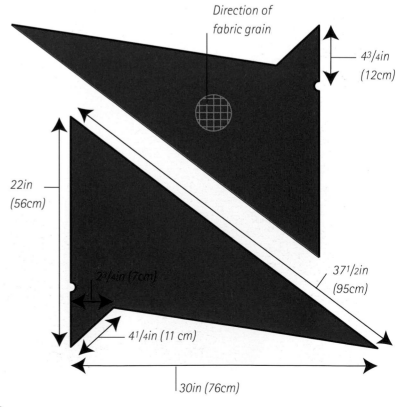

YOU WILL NEED

40in (1m) x 1½–2oz/sq yd (40–60g/sq m) ripstop nylon

5½ft (1.66m) x 3/16-in (4mm)-diameter carbon-fiber rod

4 x 3/16-in (4mm) leading-edge connectors

1 x 3/16 in (4mm) T connector

8 x 3/16-in (4mm) vinyl end caps

2 x 1/10-in (2mm) sail holders

2 x 1/10-in (2mm) spar holders

2yds (2m) x 2-in (5cm)-wide Dacron tape

20-in (50cm) x 1-in (2.5cm)-wide Dacron tape

16-in (40cm) x 1/10-in (2mm) carbon-fiber rod

15ft (4.5m) x 80-lb (36kg) braided flying line

2 x 1/2-in (12mm) alloy rings

3/4in (2cm) x 1¼-in(4mm)-diameter clear plastic tubing

Soldering iron

Pencil

Measuring tape

Scissors

1 *The sail is made from two pieces of nylon joined down the center (which uses the minimum amount of fabric). Mark the fabric by drawing the center line; then mark the wingtip points, followed by the indent points. Also mark the center cutout point. Once this is complete, check that all your measurements and angles are correct, then cut out the sail.*

There is 5/8in (1.5cm) allowed for the hem on the trailing edge.

Turn this over and machine stitch it. Then join the two halves of the sail along the center line, with a 5/8-in (1.5cm) rolled seam. (See Step 3, page 105.)

Direction of fabric grain

4¾in (12cm)

22in (56cm)

2¾in (7cm)

37½in (95cm)

4¼in (11 cm)

30in (76cm)

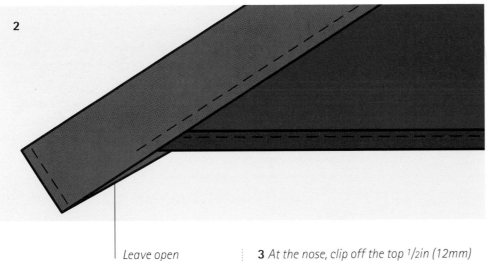

Leave open

2 The leading-edge binding is made from 2-in (5cm)-wide Dacron tape folded in half, which binds the main sail material to form a pocket for the spars. When sewing on these sleeves, start at the wingtip and work toward the nose. Leave a small gap at the wingtip so that you can insert the spars when you assemble the kite: see diagram for exact construction.

Cut off excess
above this line

3 At the nose, clip off the top 1/2in (12mm) to make a blunt shape. Make a pocket (for the spine) from 1-in (2.5cm) Dacron tape to the back of the sail. (See Step 5, page 106, on how to make a pocket.) Stitch the pocket to the nose of the sail, so that its open end points down the middle of the kite. Then fold a piece of 2-in (5cm) Dacron tape in half over the top of this pocket and the leading-edge sleeves to reinforce the nose. Stitch it in place down each side, but not along the bottom, so that the spine pocket is left open.

4 Sew a 2-in (5cm)-square patch of Dacron tape around the center cutout to reinforce this area. Then make the center hole, using a soldering iron to melt through the patch and the nylon beneath.

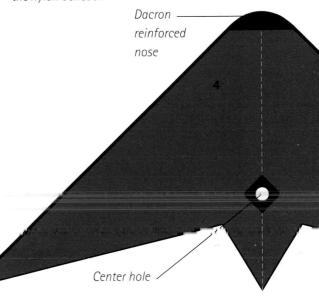

Dacron
reinforced
nose

Center hole

5 Make a pocket from 1-in (2.5cm) Dacron tape. Stitch it to the tail end of the center line for the spine, on the back of the kite.

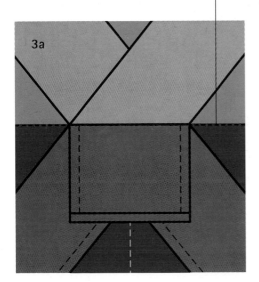

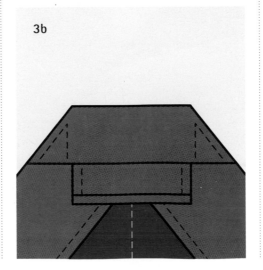

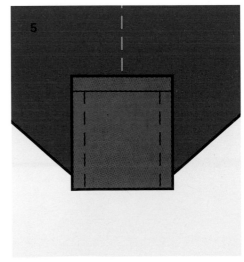

6 *Stitch on the stand-off reinforcement patches. Use 1¼in (3cm) of 1-in (2.5cm)-wide Dacron tape folded in half. Make a small hole in the center of each, using the tip of a soldering iron.*

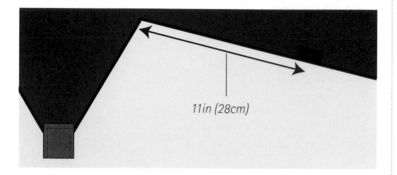

11in (28cm)

7 *Mark and cut out the holes in the leading edges for the cross spar connectors. That completes the sail. As a final check, fold it in half and make sure that it is reasonably symmetrical: the wingtips should be within 2in (5cm) of each other.*

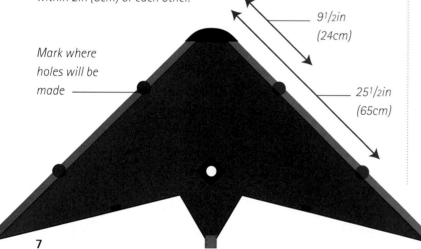

Mark where holes will be made

9¹/2in (24cm)

25¹/2in (65cm)

7

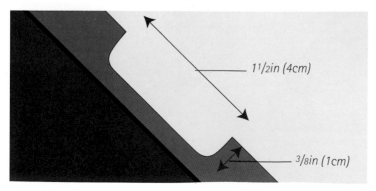

1¹/2in (4cm)

³/8in (1cm)

8 *Using the completed sail to give you the required size, cut the spine. The fit should be tight, as the sail will stretch when you fly the kite. Always cut the longest spars first. Then assemble the spine. Fit the end caps and center T connector and then fit the spine into the pockets on the back of the kite.*

9 *Push the T connector through the central cutout. Cut the spars for the leading edge, again using the kite to determine the length. Assemble the leading edges: each spar has two end caps and connectors to be slid into place.*

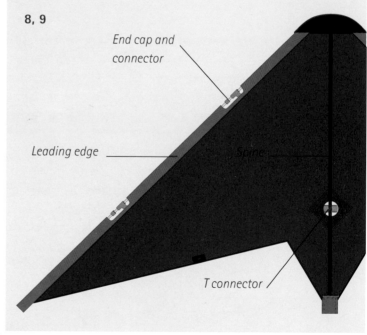

8, 9

End cap and connector

Leading edge

Spine

T connector

10 *Cut the bottom cross spars to size – 20in (50cm) – and fit them into place. Then fit and cut the stand-offs to size – 5¹/2in (14cm) or longer if required. They should pull the sail out tight. Fit a sail holder and a spar holder to each end of the stand-off. Cut and fit the top cross spar, 14in (36cm) long.*

Sail holder   Spar holder

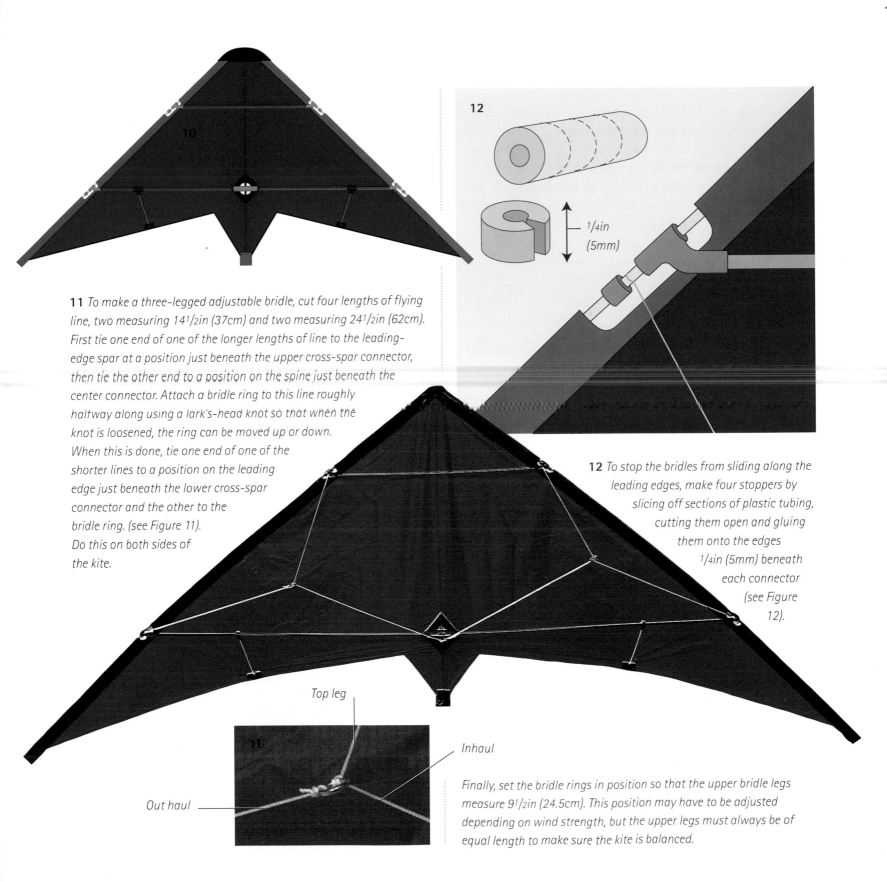

11 To make a three-legged adjustable bridle, cut four lengths of flying line, two measuring 14$\frac{1}{2}$in (37cm) and two measuring 24$\frac{1}{2}$in (62cm). First tie one end of one of the longer lengths of line to the leading-edge spar at a position just beneath the upper cross-spar connector, then tie the other end to a position on the spine just beneath the center connector. Attach a bridle ring to this line roughly halfway along using a lark's-head knot so that when the knot is loosened, the ring can be moved up or down. When this is done, tie one end of one of the shorter lines to a position on the leading edge just beneath the lower cross-spar connector and the other to the bridle ring. (see Figure 11). Do this on both sides of the kite.

12 To stop the bridles from sliding along the leading edges, make four stoppers by slicing off sections of plastic tubing, cutting them open and gluing them onto the edges 1/4in (5mm) beneath each connector (see Figure 12).

1/4in (5mm)

Top leg

Inhaul

Out haul

Finally, set the bridle rings in position so that the upper bridle legs measure 9$\frac{1}{2}$in (24.5cm). This position may have to be adjusted depending on wind strength, but the upper legs must always be of equal length to make sure the kite is balanced.

Soft stunter

Many soft stunters are notoriously difficult to make. This is usually due to the large number of bridle lines that have to be individually adjusted to make the kite fly. However, this design avoids adjustment by using a combination of reflexed sections and small keels to set the flying angle automatically. Once you have sewn it together, it is easy to set up, but the construction is a little complex and is best attempted by someone who is experienced on a sewing machine.

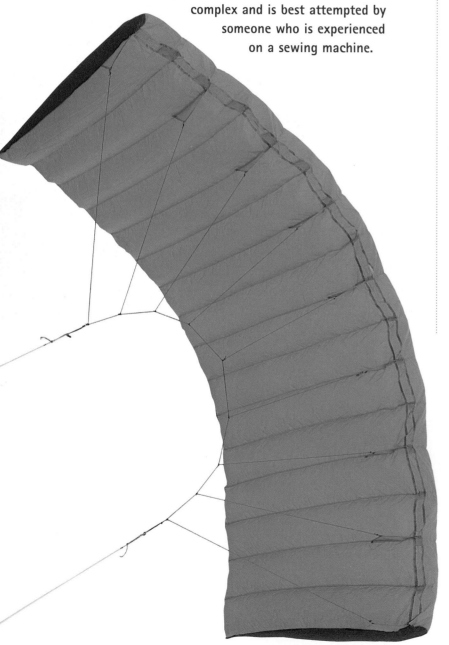

YOU WILL NEED

Large pieces of heavy paper or cardboard (for templates)

6¾yd (6m) ripstop nylon

17yd (15m) x 100-lb (45kg) braided line

Polyester sewing thread

Sharp scissors

Measuring tape

Pencil

1 *Make templates from cardboard or heavy paper for the triangular keels and wing ribs. They should correspond exactly to the measurements shown on the diagrams. Use the templates and a pencil to mark the shapes on the ripstop nylon. There should be nine triangular keels and seventeen wing ribs. Cut out the shapes.*

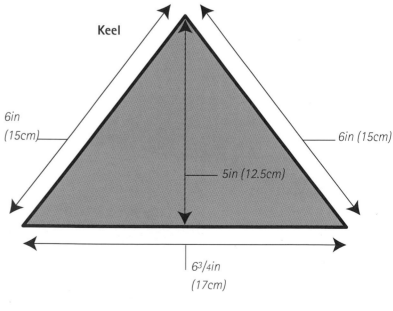

Keel

6in (15cm) — 6in (15cm)

5in (12.5cm)

6¾in (17cm)

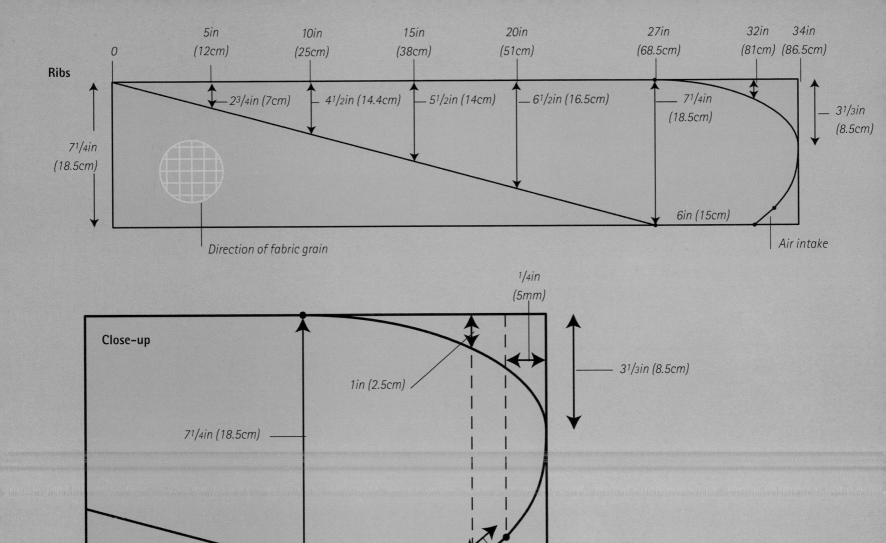

Ribs

5in (12cm) 10in (25cm) 15in (38cm) 20in (51cm) 27in (68.5cm) 32in (81cm) 34in (86.5cm)

0

2³⁄₄in (7cm) 4¹⁄₂in (14.4cm) 5¹⁄₂in (14cm) 6¹⁄₂in (16.5cm) 7¹⁄₄in (18.5cm)

3¹⁄₃in (8.5cm)

7¹⁄₄in (18.5cm)

6in (15cm)

Direction of fabric grain

Air intake

Close-up

¹⁄₄in (5mm)

3¹⁄₃in (8.5cm)

1in (2.5cm)

7¹⁄₄in (18.5cm)

6in (15cm)

Air intake 1¹⁄₂in (4cm)

2 *The top and bottom panels of the sail are rectangles, both measuring 38¹⁄₂ x 96in (98 x 244cm). Mark and cut out two rectangles for these panels. The dotted lines on the diagram show where the wing ribs will be sewn, spaced 6in (15cm) apart. Mark these lines on each piece as a guide for sewing the ribs in place.*

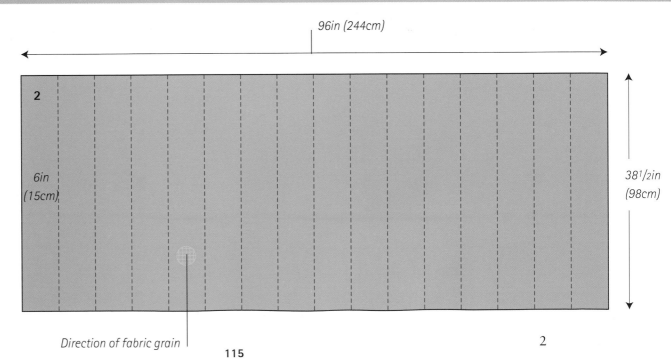

96in (244cm)

2

6in (15cm)

38¹⁄₂in (98cm)

Direction of fabric grain

2

115

3 *Each of the keels will need a nylon loop at its apex. Cut out eight loop pieces, each measuring 1¹/₂ x 2in (4 x 5cm). Hem each long side by folding over ¹/₄in (5mm) and then another ¹/₄in (5mm). Then hem the two diagonal sides of each triangle, again by folding over ¹/₄in (5mm) twice. Fold a tab piece in half over each apex and sew firmly in place.*

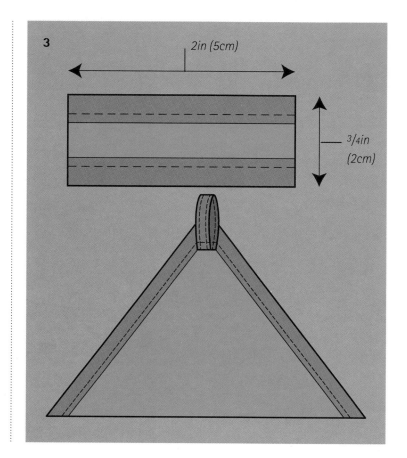

3

2in (5cm)

³/₄in
(2cm)

4 *Hem the air-intake area on each of the ribs (see diagram), again by folding over ¹/₄in (5mm) twice.*

5 *Hem the leading edge of the top and bottom panels of the sail, by folding over ¹/₄in (5mm) twice.*

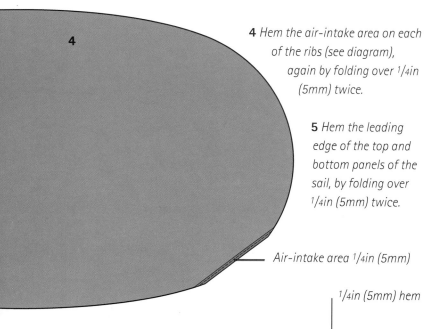

4

Air-intake area ¹/₄in (5mm)

¹/₄in (5mm) hem

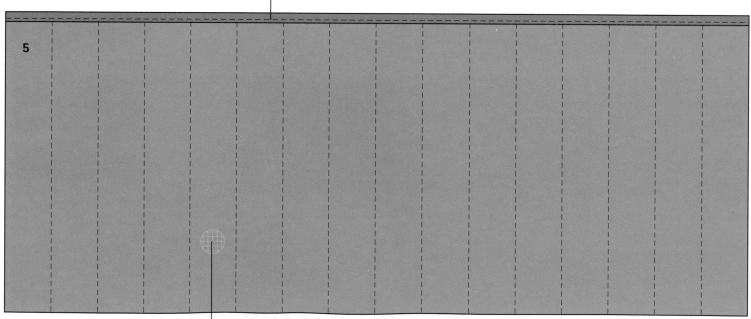

5

Direction of fabric grain

Attach keels as shown

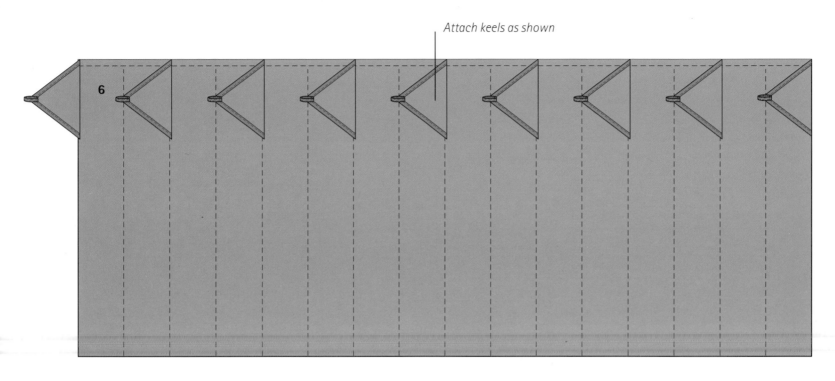

6 *Sew the keels in place on the bottom panel, allowing a ³/₈-in (1cm) seam and aligning the seams with the guidelines.*

7 *Sew the ribs into place on the other side of the bottom panel, again allowing a ³/₈-in (1cm) seam and aligning the seams with the* guidelines. *These seams follow the same lines as the keel seams, but do not catch and trap any other parts of the keels as you sew.*

Attach ribs to the other side

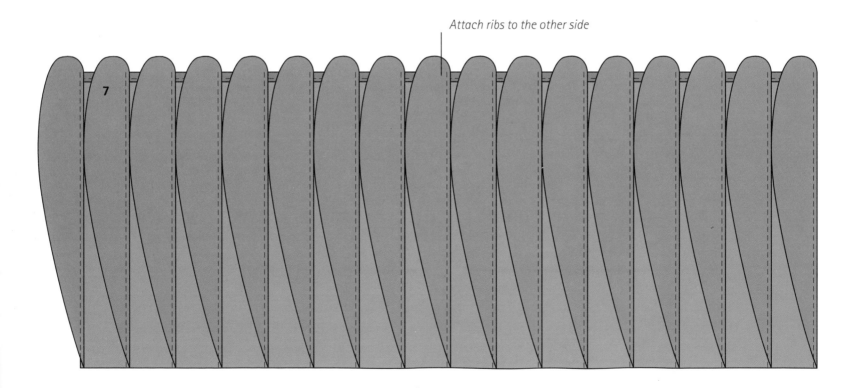

8 *Now you are ready to join the top panel to the half-assembled bottom panel. The trick is to start with all the top panel under the sewing-machine arm (on the right-hand side of the needle) and work across so that progressively less fabric is left under the arm. The last rib is finished by rolling the whole kite up and turning it inside out and then sewing the last seam in place. You turn the kite right side out by pulling the fabric out through the trailing edge.*

9 *The two long sides of the trailing edge may not align exactly. However, where they meet, sew them together with a 3/8-in (1cm) seam. Trim the longer side so that there is an extra 3/8-in (1cm) out from the other edge. Then fold this over to cover the other raw edge and fold them both over again to create a rolled seam (see step 3, page 105). Machine stitch in place.*

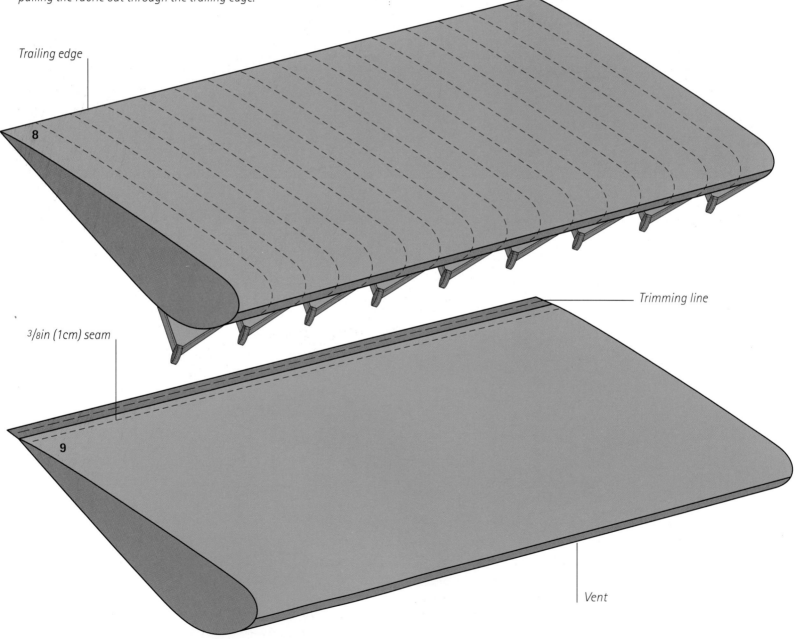

Trailing edge

8

Trimming line

3/8in (1cm) seam

9

Vent

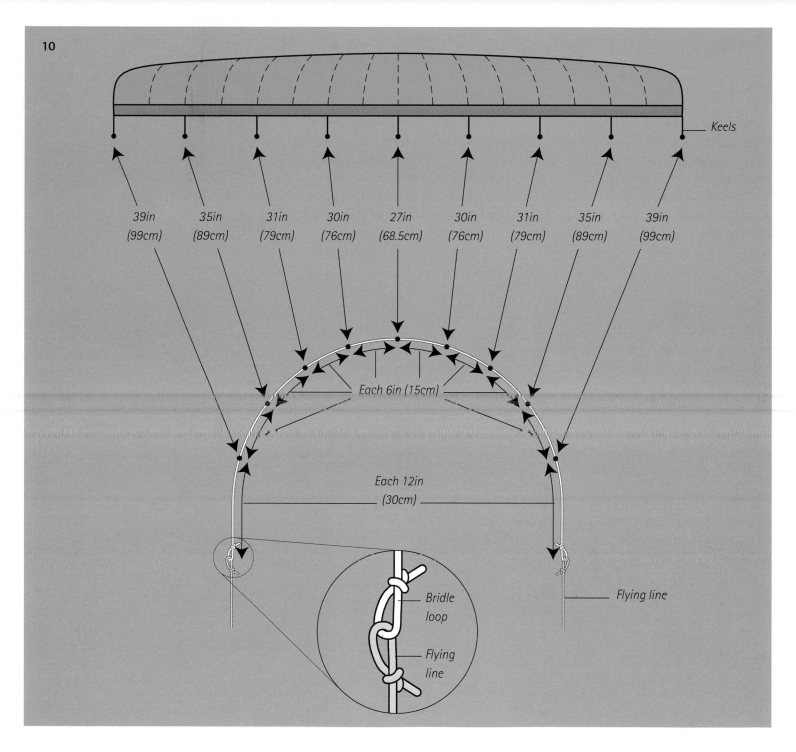

10 Keels

39in (99cm) 35in (89cm) 31in (79cm) 30in (76cm) 27in (68.5cm) 30in (76cm) 31in (79cm) 35in (89cm) 39in (99cm)

Each 6in (15cm)

Each 12in (30cm)

Bridle loop

Flying line

Flying line

10 *The kite is now finished and you are ready to make the bridle from the braided flying line. For best results, try to keep the lengths specified accurate to about ¹/2in (1cm). Cut a length 7ft (2.1m) long for the bridle arc. Fold it in half and make a 3/8-in (1cm) loop in its center. Then tie four single knots on each side of the loop at 6-in (15cm) intervals. (These knots are to stop the other knots from sliding up and down the bridle arc.) Then tie a loop at each end of the arc.*

Now cut the individual bridle lines to the lengths shown in the diagram. Tie one end of each line to the tabs on the keels and the other end on the downward side of the appropriate knot on the bridle arc. The central line is tied to the central loop on the arc.

11 *Now the kite is ready to be taken out and flown. It is self-adjusting and should need no further trimming.*

Festivals

If time and money were no object, kiters would find it possible to attend a kite festival somewhere in the world on almost every weekend of the year. These numerous events are as diverse in scale as they are in content, some constituting small gatherings of local enthusiasts and others attracting fliers from the vast international community. Kite festivals are the forums at which the devotees of kite flying share their creative skills and ideas. Furthermore, they are the aerial exhibitions mounted to celebrate the bizarre and deftly crafted toys of the wind.

Many established kite festivals feature workshops where even the uninitiated can learn kite-making and flying skills from well-seasoned experts. With a broad appeal which captivates both the active participator or the passive observer, some of today's kite festivals attract crowds that number hundreds of thousands.

Above: *This Chinese dragon makes its appearance at the Washington Tyne and Wear Festival of the Air in England.*

Above: *A preflight check is made before this car is launched into the skies at Castigilioni Kite Festival in Italy.*

Above right and right: *Customized Revolution (above right) and a modern version of Bell's tetrahedral (right) rest amid the aerial antics of the Bristol International Festival in Britain.*

Left: *A 4-ft (1.2m) Flexifoil eases into the air at the expert hands of 2¹/₂-year-old Axl Ferraro .*

Below: *Thousands share in the mayhem at the All Saints' Day kite festival in Guatemala.*

Below: *Flyers at Ostia Festival in Italy tease the wind with a play sail designed by American artist George Peters.*

Above: *American kite designer Joel Schultz displays one of his fish banners at Ostia Kite Festival.*

Above: *George Peters' kite banners create the illusion of a coral reef in the skies over Scheveningen in Holland.*

Worldwide retailers

The following specalist kite retailers will be able to provide information on local and international clubs and festivals.

AUSTRALIA

Aloft In Oz
13 Merimbula Plaza
Merimbula
NSW 2548
Tel/Fax: 064 953466

AUSTRIA

Fly High
Argentinierstr. 16
A1040 Wien
Tel/Fax: 1 50 50 260
E-mail:
  flyhigh@site86.ping.at

BELGIUM

Heaven S. P. R. L
58 Rue Des Minimes
1000 Bruxelles
Tel: 32 2 5024560
      32 2 5123596
Fax: 32 2 5123596

CANADA

Alberta Sky Scratchers
4312-46th Street
Edmonton
Alberta T6L 6L9
Tel: 403 463 3548

Island Wind & Wheels
1207 Wharf Street
Victoria
BC V8W 1T9
Tel/Fax: 604 382-KITE

On The Wind Enterprises
365 Broad Street
Regina
Saskatchewan S4R 1X2
Tel/Fax: 306 775 2988
Tel: 306 789 2276

The Kite Company
Box 81129
755 Lake Bonavista
  Drive SE
Calgary
Alberta T2J 7C9
Tel: 403 278 8598

The Kite Shop Granville
  Island
1496 Cartwright Street
Box 13
Vancouver
BC V6H 3Y5
Tel: 604 685 9877
Fax: 604 698 0820

DENMARK

Drageriet
Jaettehøjen 25
DK-8240 Risskov
Tel: 45 86 21 00 91
Fax: 45 86 21 51 10

FRANCE

ADULTS only ® /
  Sky's The Limit ®
11 rue des Romains
67200 Strasbourg
Tel: 88 29 98 64
Fax: 88 27 22 72

Le Ciel est à Tout le
  Monde
10 Rue Gay-Lussac
75005 Paris
Tel: 1 46 33 21 50
Fax: 1 44 07 25 24

GERMANY

Aero Fly Kite
Postfach 32
D-73548 Waldstetten
Tel: 7171 40950
Fax: 7171 44614

Drachennest
Bellenstr. 33
68163 Mannheim
Tel/Fax: 0621 828 1058

Edi's Drachenladen
Erbprinzenstr. 92
75175 Pforzheim
Tel: 07231 105593
Fax: 07231 356812

Fridolin's
Lister Meile 15
30161 Hannover
Tel: 0511 31 23 56
Fax: 0511 31 22 41

Höhenflug, Der
  Drachenladen
Knooper Weg 185
24118 Kiel
Tel: 431 804604
Fax: 431 802088

JAPAN

Air's Kiteworks Co, Ltd.
1-9-4 Ebisuminami
Shibuya-ku
Tokyo 150
Tel: 03 3760 7341
Fax: 03 3760 7342

Dualine Kites
OCTPIA Midorigahama
  A103
7-43 Midorigahama
Chigasaki-shi
Kanagawa 253
Tel: 0467 88 1939
Fax: 0467 86 3979

The Kite World
214 Futatsubashi-machi
Seya-ku
Yokohama-shi
Kanagawa-ken 246
Tel/Fax: 045 391 6003
E-mail:
  aodagawa@cap.
  bekkoame.or.jp

MEXICO

Pablo's Old Town Kites
18 Zaragosa
Puerto Peñasco, Sonora
Tel: 5 26 38 3 35 45

NETHERLANDS

Van Amerongen
  Sportkites Holland
"The Kite Gallery"
Damplein 9
Middelburg 4331 GC
Tel: 1180 37526
Fax: 1180 24654

Vlieger–OP
Weteringkade 5A
2515 AK The Hague
Tel: 70 385 8586
      70 383 3396
Fax: 70 383 8541
E-mail: nop@euronet.nl

NORWAY

Kites & Buggies
PO Box 4609
4616 Kristiansand S
Tel: 380 32623
Fax: 380 33957

PUERTO RICO

Caribbean Kite &
  Sport Co.
158 Flamboyan Street
Bo Esperanza
Vieques 00765
Tel: 809 741 1381

SINGAPORE

East South Enterprises
  Pte. Ltd.
20 Marina Mall,
#01–02
Marina South
019392
Tel: 065 226 0928
Fax: 065 221 3822

SPAIN

Indigo Cometas SCP
Amigo, 25
08021 Barcelona
Tel: 3 414 59 18
Fax: 3 414 59 63

SWITZERLAND

etc...
112 Aarbergstrasse
2501 Biel/Bienne
Tel: 32 232323
Fax: 32 235011

UNITED KINGDOM

Air Born Kites
42 Gardner Street
Brighton
E. Sussex BN1 1UN
Tel/Fax: 01273 676 740

Air Circus
15 High Street Arcade
Cardiff CF1 2BB
Tel: 01222 666 485

Bristol Kite Store
1B Pitville Place
Cotham Hill
Bristol BS6 6JY
Tel: 0117 974 5010
Fax: 0117 973 7202

High As A Kite
153 Stoke Newington
  Church Street
London N16 0UH
Tel: 0171 275 8799
Fax: 0171 275 8799

Kosmic Kites
161 Ewell Road
Surbiton
Surrey KT6 6AW
Tel: 0181 390 2221

Ocean Kites
Unit 43, Kingswell Path
Cascades Shopping
  Centre
Portsmouth PO1 4RR
Tel: 01705 821666

The Kite Store Ltd.
48 Neal Street
London WC2H 9PA
Tel: 0171 836 1666
Fax: 0171 372 2771

Tradewind Kites
6 Harris Arcade
Reading
Berkshire RG1 1DN
Tel/Fax: 01734 568848

Whaam! Kites
Unit 416
Lakeside Shopping
  Centre
West Thurrock
Grays
Essex RM16 1ZT
Tel/Fax: 01708 864074

Wind Things
11 Cowgatehead
Edinburgh EH1 1JY
Tel/Fax: 0131 220 6336

UNITED STATES OF
AMERICA

Air Adventures
924 E. Douglas
Wichita KS 67202
Tel: 316 265 0909
Fax: 316 265 0927

Air Apparent Kites
396 Trolley Square
Salt Lake City
UT 84102
Tel: 801 531 7434
Fax: 801 487 8775
E-mail: aakite@aol.com

Air Circus Kite Shop
1114 Boardwalk
Ocean City NJ 08226
Tel/Fax: 609 399 9343

Annie's Kites & Wind
  Things
492 Kendrick Street
Paramus NJ 07652
Tel/Fax: 201 444 4366
E-mail: arcb@aol.com

Anything That Flies
9-C Vessup Lane
St. Thomas USVI 00801
Tel: 809 776 5300

Buffalo Beano Co.
801 University Avenue
Lubbock
TX 79401-2419
Tel: 806 762 8553
        800 788-BEANO
Fax: 806 763-KITE

Chicago Kite Company
Six South Brockway
Palatine IL 60064
Tel: 708 359 2556
Fax: 708 885 7197

Colors on the Wind
118 E. Wellesley
Spokane WA 99207
Tel: 509 484-KITE

Down to Earth Kites
199 Edgewater Drive W
East Falmouth
MA 02536
Tel: 508 457 5561
        508 566 0641

Epic Kites Etc.
423 Culver Boulevard
Playa Del Rey
CA 90293
Tel: 310 822 9550

Fish Creek Kite Co.
3851 Highway 42
PO Box 331
Fish Creek WI 54212
Tel: 414 868 3769
Fax: 414 839 9260
E-mail: tschlick@mail.
  wiscnet.net

Flags & Kites
3280 So. 4th Avenue #C
Yuma AZ 85365
Tel: 520 344 1535
Fax: 520 344 3479

Flash Flights
313 63rd Street
Holmes Beach FL 34217
Tel: 941 778 7600
Fax: 941 778 7706

Fly Away Kites
1108 Main Street
Belmar NJ 07719
Tel: 908 280 8084
Fax: 908 681 0523

Gasworks Park Kite Shop/
  Goodwinds® Kites
3333 Wallingford North
Seattle WA 98103
Tel: 206 633 4780
Fax: 206 633 0301

High Flyers Flight
  Company Inc.
492 Thames Street
Newport RI 02840
Tel/Fax: 401 846 3262

High Performance Kites
1450 Ala Moana Blvd.
Honolulu HI 96814
Tel: 808 947 7097
Fax: 808 951 5483

Highline Kites
5901 San Jose Avenue
Richmond Annex
CA 94804
Tel: 510 525 2755

Into the Wind, Inc.
1408 Pearl Street
Boulder CO 80302
Tel: 303 449 5356
Fax: 303 449 7315
E-mail:
  intowind@aol.com

Island Kites
Box 59
Middle Bass OH 43446
Tel: 419 285 4173
  (Summer)
  216 333 7004 (Winter)

It Flys
1208½ Howard Street
Omaha NE 68102
Tel: 402 346 3607

Kaleidoscope
Box 695
Bellevue NE 68005
Tel: 402 292 1704
        402 292 7258

Key West Kite
  Company Inc.
409 Green Street
Key West FL 33040
Tel: 305 296 2535

Kite Flite
3615 India Street
San Diego CA 92103
Tel: 619 299 1548
Fax: 619 299 5703

Kite Flite
San Diego Seaport
  Village
839 W. Harbor Dr. #D
San Diego CA 92101
Tel: 619 234-KITE

Kite Flite
Pier 39, Space B-12
San Francisco CA 94133
Tel: 415 956 3181

Kite Harbor
109 North Marion
Oak Park IL 60301
Tel: 708 848 4907
Fax: 312 321 5484

Kite Koop, Inc.
6176 Landmark Plaza
PO Box 242
Chincoteague Island
VA 23336
Tel: 804 336 5554
Fax: 804 336 1762

Kite Kraft
576 South Main
Frankenmuth MI 48734
Tel: 517 652 2961

Kites & Fun Things Ltd
1049 South Main
Plymouth MI 48170
Tel: 313 454 3760
Fax: 313 454 0345

Kites & More
5604 Menaul Blvd NE
Albuquerque NM 87110
Tel: 505 883 0028

Kites Unlimited
Atlantic Station
  Shopping Center
PO Box 2278
Atlantic Beach
NC 28512-2278
Tel: 919 247 7011

Kitty Hawk Kites
Bypass 158, Mile Post
  13
PO Box 1839
Nags Head NC 27959
Tel: 919 441 4124
Fax: 919 441 7597
E-mail:
  khhinfo@interpath.com

Klig's Kites
811-C Seaboard Street
Myrtle Beach SC 29577
Tel: 803 448 7881
        803 449 2856
Fax: 803 448 7370

Mackinaw Kite Co.
116 Washington Street
Grand Haven MI 49417
Tel: 616 846 7501

Nevada Kite & Ski
947 North Pecos Road
Las Vegas NV 89101
Tel: 702 642 0254
Fax: 702 399 4994

Northwind Kites, Inc.
Fifth Avenue Mall
320 West 5th Avenue
Suite 156
Anchorage AK 99501
Tel: 907 279 4386
Fax 907 279 4388

Ocean Kites
511 Pacific Avenue S.
PO Box 1287
Long Beach WA 98631
Tel: 360 642 2229
        360 642 8988
Fax: 360 642 8986

Paint The Sky Kites
828 NW 23rd Avenue
Portland OR 97210
Tel: 503 222 5096
Fax: 503 222 5034
E-mail: bugjon@aol.com

Play With The Wind
1306 North Eclipse
  Place
South Bend IN 46628
Tel: 219 237 0395
        800 946 3321
Fax: 219 237 0395
E-mail:
  kestrel511@aol.com

Shoot the Breeze
1530 Cumberland
  Terrace
Acworth
GA 30102-1336
Tel: 404 928 3468

Sky's The Limit
#5 The Courtyard
Nantucket MA 02554
Tel: 508 228 4633
Fax: 508 228 1452

Sodbuster's Sky Toys
105 South Polk
PO Box 569
Pleasantville IA 50225
Tel: 515 848 5686

Stanton Hobby Shop, Inc.
4718 N. Milwaukee Ave.
Chicago IL 60630
Tel: 312 283 6446
Fax: 312 283 6842

The Kite Hangar
4789 Summerhurst
  Drive
Liverpool NY 13088
Tel: 315 457 6000
        800 70-KITES

The Kite Loft of New
  Orleans, Inc.
Riverwalk, Space 90
1 Poydras
New Orleans LA 70130
Tel: 504 529 3247
Fax: 504 566 0730

The Kite Loft of
  Ocean City, Inc.
511 Boardwalk
PO Box 551
Ocean City, MD 21842
Tel: 410 289 7855
        410 289 6852
Fax: 410 289 5726
E-mail:
  JayK100000@aol.com

Unique Place—World
  of Kites
525 S. Washington
Royal Oak MI 48067
Tel: 810 398 5900
        810 356 1427

USA Kites
272 Dixon Avenue
Pittsburgh PA 15216
Tel: 412 561 8785

Wind & Sky
PO Box 34757
Juneau AK 99803
Tel: 907 789 0200
Fax: 907 789 1667

Windborne Kites
585 Cannery Row #105
Monterey CA 93940
Tel: 408 373 7422
Fax: 408 373 0688

Wings
3220 Oxford Lane NW
Rochester MN 55901
Tel: 507 288 0145

Wings On Strings
1141 SE Grand #114
Oklahoma City
OK 73129
Tel/Fax: 405 670 2221

Wings on the Wind
110 W. Wooster Street
Bowling Green
OH 43402
Tel: 419 352-KITE

Wizard of the Wind
13761 Braun Drive
Golden CO 80401
Tel: 303 478 6394

Index

(numbers in italics refer to illustrations)